AF470328

BERYL COOK 1926-2008

First edition published in the UK in 2008 by University of Plymouth Press, Scott Building, Drake Circus, Plymouth, Devon, PL4 8AA, United Kingdom.

Published on the occasion of the Beryl Cook 1926-2008 exhibition, 8 November 2008 - 20 December 2008. University of Plymouth, Peninsula Arts Gallery, Drake Circus, Plymouth, Devon, PL4 8AA, United Kingdom.

uppress.co.uk/berylcook.htm

Editors: Jess Wilder and Sarah Chapman
Consulting Editor: Liz Wells
Publisher: Paul Honeywill

A catalogue record of this book is available from the British Library

ISBN: 978-1-84102-195-9

Library of Congress Cataloging in Publication

Printed and bound by Deltor Limited, Plymouth.

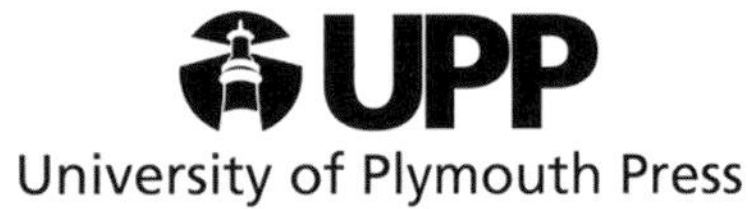

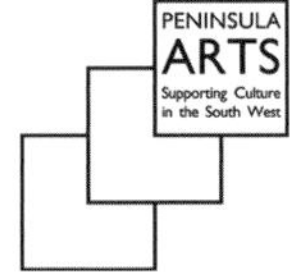

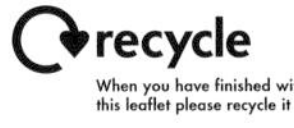

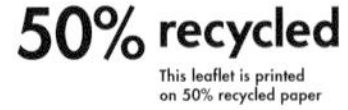

CONTENTS

FOREWORD

This special book, *Beryl Cook, 1926–2008*, catalogues the artist's work and offers critical commentary and broad reassessment of Beryl Cook's remarkable position in British popular culture. It has been published on the occasion of a unique exhibition at Peninsula Arts Gallery, University of Plymouth, featuring more than 70 of her pieces, including many rarely seen as well as her best-known paintings. Beryl Cook was one of the UK's best-loved and most successful contemporary artists. Most people are familiar with her larger-than-life depictions of men and women going about their daily lives, portrayed with her unmistakable humour and charm. It is fitting that Plymouth, the city that was her home for 40 years and inspired many of her paintings, should host this major event.

This book showcases her work and also reveals her more personal paintings, including family portraits. It is a celebration of her artistic achievement, which won her millions of fans around the world.

Contributors to the book include Bernard Samuels, who is credited with discovering Beryl in the 1970s when he was Director of the Plymouth Arts Centre, and who provides a unique insight into Plymouth's vibrant arts scene; author, poet and art critic Edward Lucie-Smith, author Babs Horton, Royal Literary Fund Writing Fellow at the University of Plymouth, who reflects on Beryl's wide popularity and appeal; Jess Wilder, co-director of London's Portal Gallery, which has shown Beryl Cook's paintings almost exclusively for 30 years and the academic and cultural theorist, Bernadette Casey.

Planning for the exhibition and book was enthusiastically supported by Beryl's husband, John Cook, their son, and friends, who loaned Peninsula Arts some rarely seen works, including personal portraits and several three-dimensional pieces such as chairs that Beryl painted and dolls that she made.

Beryl Cook died in May 2008. She was delighted that the University of Plymouth, was planning a major exhibition of her work which has become a celebration of her life as well as her artistic achievement.

Peninsula Arts operates from within the Faculty of Arts and serves as the Arts and Culture programming umbrella organisation for the University of Plymouth. The year round public programme includes exhibitions, music, film, talks and performing arts. Its aim is to provide a prestigious and wide-ranging series of events which open up the Arts and the University to the people of Plymouth and to people from across the South West of England.

Simon Ible
Director, Peninsula Arts

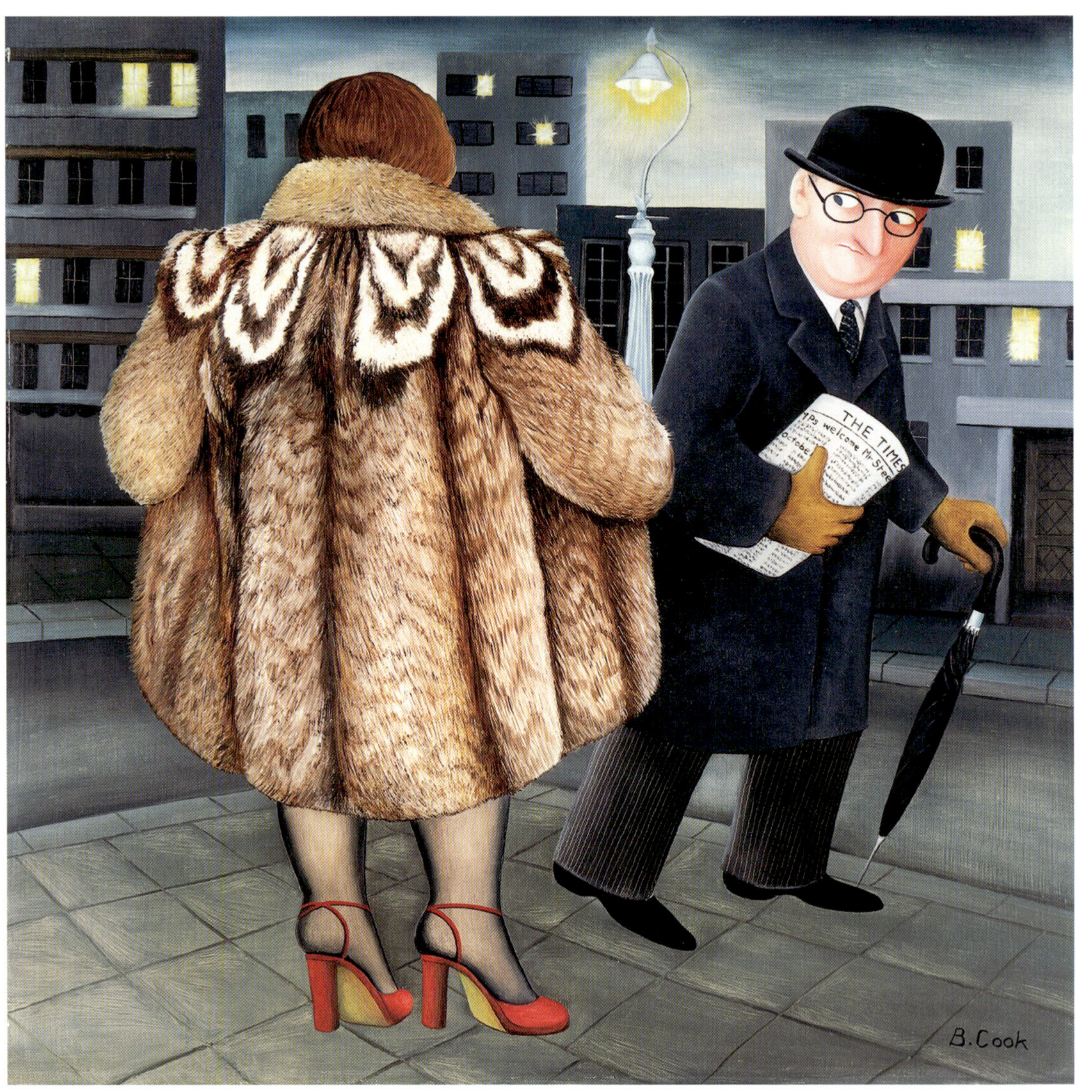

My Fur Coat
1978

BERYL COOK, 1926-2008

Jess Wilder

Beryl Cook changed the way we look at the world. It is a tribute to her fame that when we see curvaceous girls all dolled up to go out on a hen night, or a pair of plump ladies gossiping over cups of tea and enormous cream cakes Beryl Cook is the artist who comes into our minds. Life is full of such 'Beryl Cook Moments'. Her perspicacious observations have become an integral part of British life. However very few people know very much about the artist who never sought publicity, never attended one of her own private views and who only gave interviews reluctantly. Ironically, in her rare appearances on television, she came over as a natural – articulate, amusing and totally unpretentious.

Beryl Lansley was born in Egham in Surrey in 1926; four years later her parents separated. Beryl, her mother and four sisters moved to Reading and they lived next door to a boy called John Cook. Beryl left school at 14 having shown no particular interest in art. In 1944, the family moved to London where Beryl took a number of jobs: as a showgirl in a touring production of 'The Gypsy Princess' and as a model for Goldberg's of Bond Street. In 1947, they moved to Hampton, just south-west of London, to a house by the river which they ran as a tea-garden.

John Cook and Beryl met up again after the war. By then John was an officer in the Merchant Navy. They married in 1948 and their son, also named John, was born two years later. John left the Navy and briefly they ran a pub on the Essex – Suffolk border but found quite soon that country life was definitely not for them. It is clear from Beryl's paintings that the city, and all it has to offer, has always been her inspiration.

In 1956, the Cooks moved to what was then Southern Rhodesia; John worked in the motor trade and Beryl took various jobs. One day in 1960, John bought Beryl a set of oil paints, as she had become interested in painting while teaching her son. The result of this first foray into paint was the now famous – or infamous – painting of a lady with large pendulous bosoms. It was copied from a photograph and immediately entitled 'Hangover' by John. Beryl was pleased with the result, but did no more paintings until her return to England.

The Cooks moved back from Rhodesia in 1965 and bought a cottage in East Looe in Cornwall. Beryl started to paint on pieces of driftwood. In 1968, the Cooks moved to Plymouth where they bought a guest house on the Hoe. John continued to work in the motor business, and Beryl took in guests in the summer months. In the winter she began to paint again with a passion using every piece of wood she could find – lavatory seats, fire screens, wardrobe doors or driftwood. Beryl said of this time: "I had to stop painting for about four months each summer when the visitors were here, and in a way this was quite a relief for by this time there were so many paintings it had become increasingly difficult to stack them!"[1]

In the early 1970's, Beryl's paintings found their first buyers. Tony Martin, an antiques dealer friend who had bought the Cook's cottage in Looe, was very encouraging and sold some of Beryl's work; this began to give her confidence.

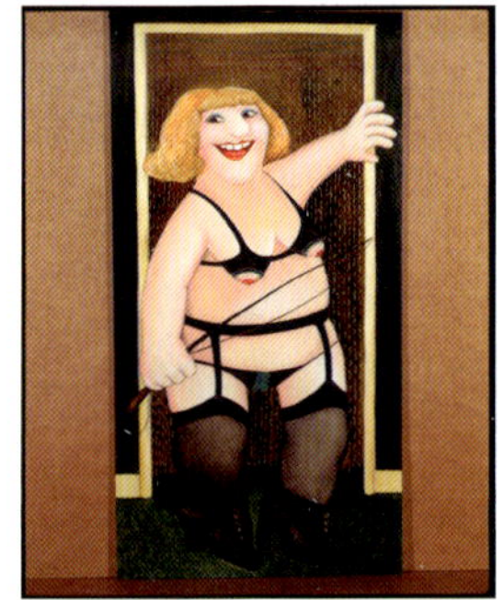

Fig. 2 Beryl Cook
Anyone for a Whipping?
Private collection

Spurred on by this success, Beryl soon covered every wall of the boarding house with her paintings, life in Plymouth proving hugely inspirational – people on the beach, a couple in a bus shelter primly eating fish and chips with filthy graffiti written up behind them. The wonderful and now iconic 'Sabotage' dates from this period. It is a painting of three bowling ladies posed in a circle. One stout lady is bending over to bowl, while her wicked companion is giving a conspiratorial look to the viewer and firmly goosing her. Beryl's natural method of composition is circular, but in this picture it is all the more apparent as it is painted directly on a round breadboard. At around this time Beryl asked John what he would like for Christmas, and he requested a lovely plump lady. 'Anyone for a Whipping?' was the result and

1 *Beryl Cook : The Works*. London: John Murray, 1977.

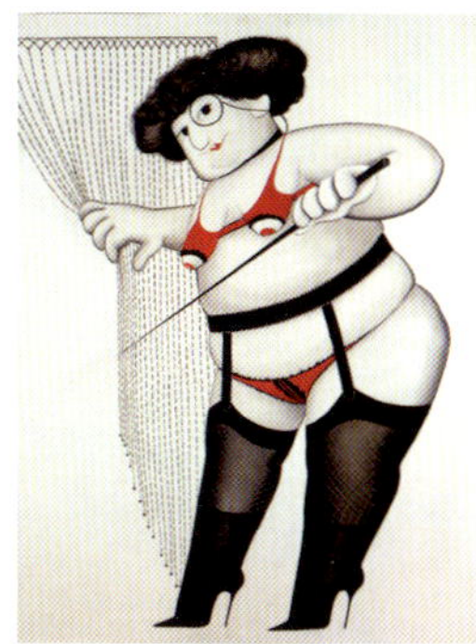

Fig. 3 Beryl Cook
Next!
Oil on panel
Private collection

makes a fine companion piece to 'Next!', a painting inspired by the film *Personal Services* based on the life of the famous South West London madam, Cynthia Payne.

Beryl's career took a further leap in the mid 1970s when an actor who was a regular guest at the Cook's boarding house told Bernard Samuels, who ran the Plymouth Art Centre, about the landlady with the house full of amazing paintings. Bernard went to see the work and with some difficulty persuaded Beryl to have an exhibition. He said he thought it would be nice for her if all the paintings could be seen together in one show as there were about 60 works. Beryl replied typically that yes, it would be nice as long as she did not have to take part in any publicity or put in an appearance. The exhibition took place in November and December 1975 and was a resounding success. Half the paintings were for sale between £40 to £60; business was brisk and the exhibition was extended longer than planned due to the huge number of visitors.

Early in 1976 *The Sunday Times* colour supplement featured 'The Lockyer Tavern' on its cover with an accompanying article 'The Paintings of a Seaside Landlady'. The Lockyer Tavern and the Dolphin on the Barbican are the Plymouth pubs that have featured most regularly in Beryl's paintings. The painting of The Lockyer shows Beryl's natural sense of composition, as she resolves a complicated scene seemingly effortlessly.

One look at her meticulously detailed sketchbooks, however, shows how painstakingly she sketched out a picture, often squaring the paper before carefully drawing it out on the surface of the wooden panel. In 'The Lockyer Tavern' we meet a few typical Beryl Cook characters: the two regulars who are waiting for the pub's gay bar to open are riveted by the barmaid who is giving some pretty colourful back-chat to an off-stage drinker. Accessories such as the 'Dame Edna Everage spectacles' worn by the lady on the left, and the bobbly plastic earrings and bracelet worn by the barmaid assure Beryl's place as a social historian and minute observer of fashion. The careful arrangement of the bottles behind the bar, and the particular shade of blue eye shadow worn by the girls, show Beryl's eye for detail.

The Dolphin Pub is the background for 'Hen Party 1' where a joyful group of girls are going into the pub. Beryl says: "The friends make the bride a hat (in this case a large cardboard box covered in silver paper and saucy decorations) and there is much singing and hooting as they go through the streets."[2] Again Beryl records the minute detail of a social ritual at a particular time.

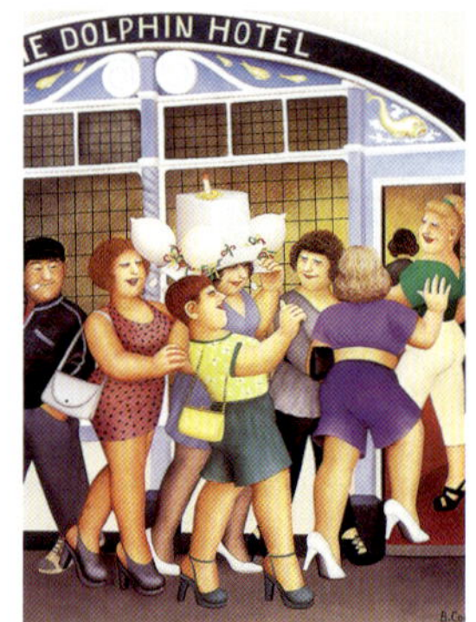

Fig. 4 Beryl Cook
Hen Party 1
Oil on panel
Private collection

Immediately after seeing *The Sunday Times* article, Lionel Levy of London's Portal Gallery telephoned Beryl, and her first London exhibition with Portal took place in 1977. What was to be her last exhibition, the eighteenth with the gallery, was in 2006 entitled 'Beryl Cook at 80'. It was a huge success.

Cook's fame grew quickly: through limited edition prints and greetings cards of her paintings, many people who had not seen the original paintings became aware of her work. In 1979, ITV's 'The South Bank Show' featured her work, and she appeared on BBC 2's 'One Pair of Eyes' in 1982. John Murray, publishers of Lord Byron and Jane Austen, brought out *Beryl Cook: The Works* in 1978 with 'Sabotage' on the cover. They went on to publish a further five books of Beryl's paintings.

Beryl's family appear quite often, particularly in the early paintings. 'Sunbathing', painted *circa* 1974, shows Beryl, her daughter-in-law and her granddaughter lying in the back garden surrounded by the cats, the tortoises and the dachshund, who is having a quick cup of tea on the sly. The composition is complicated and imaginative, and the way the figures are placed among the luxurious greenery shows an increasing confidence. 'Feeding the Tortoises' and 'Teresa in a Fox Fur' are two other similarly humorous 'family' paintings.

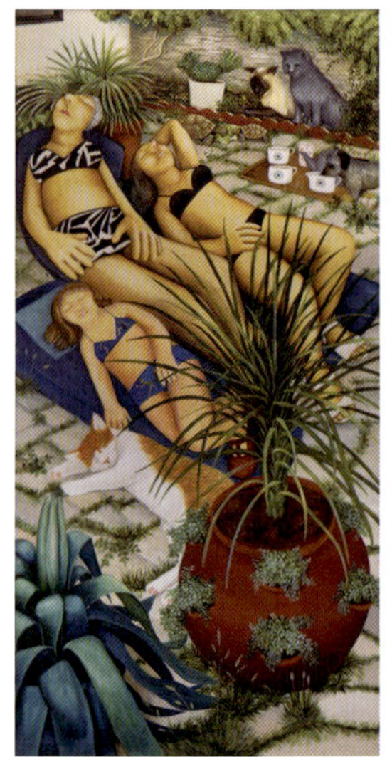

Fig. 5 Beryl Cook
Sunbathing
Oil on panel
Private collection

Beryl's increasing fame led to a number of long and special friendships. Soon after her first exhibition Beryl received a fan letter from the photographer, Barbara Ker-Seymer, who had seen her on 'The South Bank Show'. Barbara was a well-known portrait photographer whose career began in the 1930s and spanned several decades. She moved in 'bohemian' circles and had photographed glamorous actors and artists both before and after the war. 'Bar and Barbara' shows Barbara Ker Seymer and her friend dressed for New York winter going into the bar of the famous Algonquin Hotel. She and Beryl kept up a lively correspondence for many years. Barbara had shown some cards of

2 *Beryl Cook: The Bumper Edition*, edited by Joe Whitlock Blundell. London: Victor Gollancz, 2000.

Beryl's paintings to the artist Edward Burra with whom she had been at art school; he loved them. Beryl was a huge admirer of Edward Burra and also of Stanley Spencer, both of whom profoundly influenced her painting, Spencer for his compositions and bulky figures and Burra for his style and subject matter. It was Edward Burra's paintings that led Beryl and John to visit the bars around the docks in Marseilles, and to visit the cafés and night-clubs off the Ramblas in Barcelona. The stunning 'Red Umbrella' was painted after seeing this splendid lady of the night, who was a well-known sight, plying her trade at the less glamorous end of this famous street.

Beryl's paintings indicate her enjoyment of travel and socialising. She had a long correspondence with Faith Stewart Gordon, the owner of the Russian Tea Room in New York. Beryl and John visited her there and Beryl's acutely observed painting of this famous restaurant appeared in '*Beryl Cook's New York*' in 1985. Edward Lucie-Smith, the art critic, was an early champion of Beryl's work and purchased one of her earlier works. Daniel Farson, journalist, photographer and notorious Soho character, loved to go out with John and Beryl to the Dolphin or to Muriel's (The Colony Room in Soho). The Cooks usually made their exit just before things became too riotous!

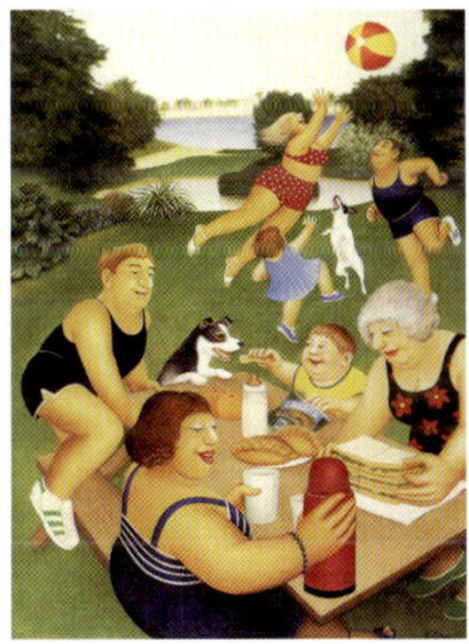

Fig. 6 Beryl Cook
Picnic at Mount Edgecumbe
Oil on panel
Private collection

Yet Beryl took much of her inspiration from Plymouth. In 'Punks on the Hoe' she portrays the clothes and hairstyles of a very particular era. Beryl's love of clothes, outrageous shoes and hairstyles made her an important chronicler of changing local fashions. In 'Doing the Lambada' Beryl paints girls performing a dance which was probably a short-lived fashion, but has been recorded for posterity by Beryl's unerring eye. In 'Picnic at Mount Edgecumbe' Beryl portrays a well known local park and picnic spot, an enthusiastic lady in a polka dot bikini jumps for a ball. Beryl has put her dog, Minnie, into the painting and he is having a wonderful time. In the foreground, a family tuck into a picnic with relish. A local touch is the very plump Cornish pasties.

Beryl and John not only travelled to the States and Europe, but in 1994, prompted by a new-found fascination for the tango, they went to Buenos Aires where they went to tango shows every night, and to the famous San Telmo Square which is an area where couples come to dance the tango outdoors. 'Tango Bar' shows a supremely confident couple in a classic tango pose – you can almost hear the accordion. The woman in her gorgeous red dress and perfect make-up gives the man a smouldering look. He is poised and in control, sporting a bold chalk-striped suit and wearing his hat at a jaunty angle. A very smartly dressed couple look on admiringly. The scene takes place on a black and white squared dance floor, and this bold pattern sets off the rest of the composition.

'Tango Busking' shows a scene outside a pavement café. The bold pattern of the woman's red dress contrasts with the men's white suits, again in the classic tango pose. Her partner, sporting a red flower behind his ear is quite carried away by the experience. The painting is a complicated composition of the street posters behind and the singer who points to the sky behind the accordionist. All the figures fit together to make a very satisfying group.

Another joyous theme which pervades Beryl's work throughout the decades is food and drink. 'Dining Out' was painted for one of Portal Gallery's themed Christmas exhibitions, Eat Drink and be Merry; this was an ideal subject for Beryl. The scene is London's Langan's Brasserie, a favourite with Beryl and John. The exuberance of the lady juggling with the champagne bottles is typical of Beryl's joyful take on the world, and the vicarious pleasure of someone giving way to the hidden extrovert appeals to us all. There are enjoyable details such as the approving glances of her companions, the disapproving look of the waiter thinking they will never leave and bearing away yet another bottle, while under the table we can see the 'co-respondent' shoes of someone who has been totally overcome by it all. 'Ladies Doing Lunch', painted in 2003, nearly 10 years later, portrays a feast: two ladies dressed up to the nines in a pub enjoying fish and chips, one with fag and beer bottle, the other carefully applying her lipstick, her mouth cunningly reflected in her mirror gives the painting a strangely surreal twist.

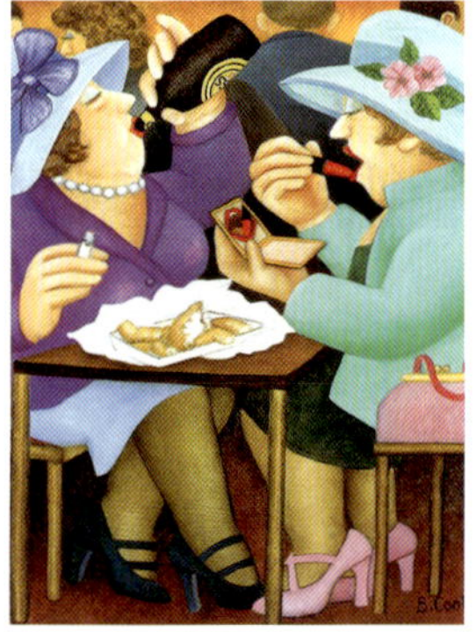

Fig. 7 Beryl Cook
Ladies Doing Lunch
Oil on panel
Private collection

Musicians were always a great favourite with Beryl. She would often listen to jazz while painting. 'The Bijou Trio' is one of Beryl's finest musician paintings, a great composition which is full of life. The double-bass player and the pianist seem to have taken over the painting leaving the exuberant lady drummer with a slightly undersized drum kit. 'Bernie and the Vibes' is another painting with music as its theme. Much time was spent finding the right illustration of a vibraphone, and here it is in all its glory with Bernie a virtuoso and regular at Langan's Brasserie. The quartet of musicians, eyes closed, are playing with such obvious enjoyment. Beryl is never tempted to caricature; her people are always completely real.

Critics have often found it difficult to place Beryl Cook. Though entirely self-taught, she is no primitive painter. Beryl's roots are much closer to artists such as Stanley Spencer and Edward Burra. She has recorded aspects of British life some years later than L.S. Lowry, and though stylistically miles apart, their touching comments on the lives of British people, and their idiosyncratic vision, have made their works instantly recognisable. Beryl's was a truly unique talent; no one painted like her.

Where does this place Beryl in art history? She was, without doubt, a consummate chronicler of (mainly British) life in the second half of the twentieth century. She was a recorder of fashion, observing subtle changes in clothes, hairstyles and shoes. She was a social historian but a painter who never caricatured – she was no Hogarth or Gilray – and she painted with compassion and a wry humour, never with cruelty. There are genuinely poignant moments in Beryl's paintings. She painted everything that interested and amused her; she was an artist of great integrity and never went for the cheap laugh. Each painting was the complex and painstaking result of an acutely observed moment, which then became a sketch, a drawing and finally a painting. Beryl, like all artists, suffered from the disappointment that is the gulf between the original idea and what is finally expressed in the painting. Beryl was never totally satisfied with the result, and this spurred her on to paint the next one. She was a much more serious artist than her subject matter would suggest.

Beryl Cook was awarded the OBE for services to art in 1996, and her paintings have been acquired by Glasgow's Museum of Modern Art, Bristol City Art Gallery and Durham Art Gallery. Her paintings also hang in significant collections around the world. Portal Gallery, London, represents Beryl's work. Our long association, of over 30 years, has been a very happy one. Beryl Cook was a friend, warm hearted and kind and a joy to work with. She had a great gift and gave so many people all over the world great pleasure. The press coverage on her death in May 2008 was overwhelming, with obituaries and affectionate and serious appreciations on the front pages of all the national dailies and the centre pages of *The Sun*!

There was a major retrospective at the Baltic in Gateshead in 2007, and this book is being published to coincide with a long overdue retrospective, in Autumn 2008, of Beryl's work in her home town, Plymouth, bringing together over 70 major works including some truly iconic paintings such as 'My Fur Coat', 'Queen of the Fairies' and 'Percy at the Fridge'. This exhibition was designed as the largest collection of Beryl Cook's work shown together to date.

Jess Wilder is co-director of Portal Gallery, London.
Portal Gallery has exhibited and sold Beryl Cook's paintings since 1976.
www.berylcook.org

A version of this essay has previously been published in *The World of Beryl Cook* edited by Jerome Sans & Jess Wilder. London: Prestel, 2007.

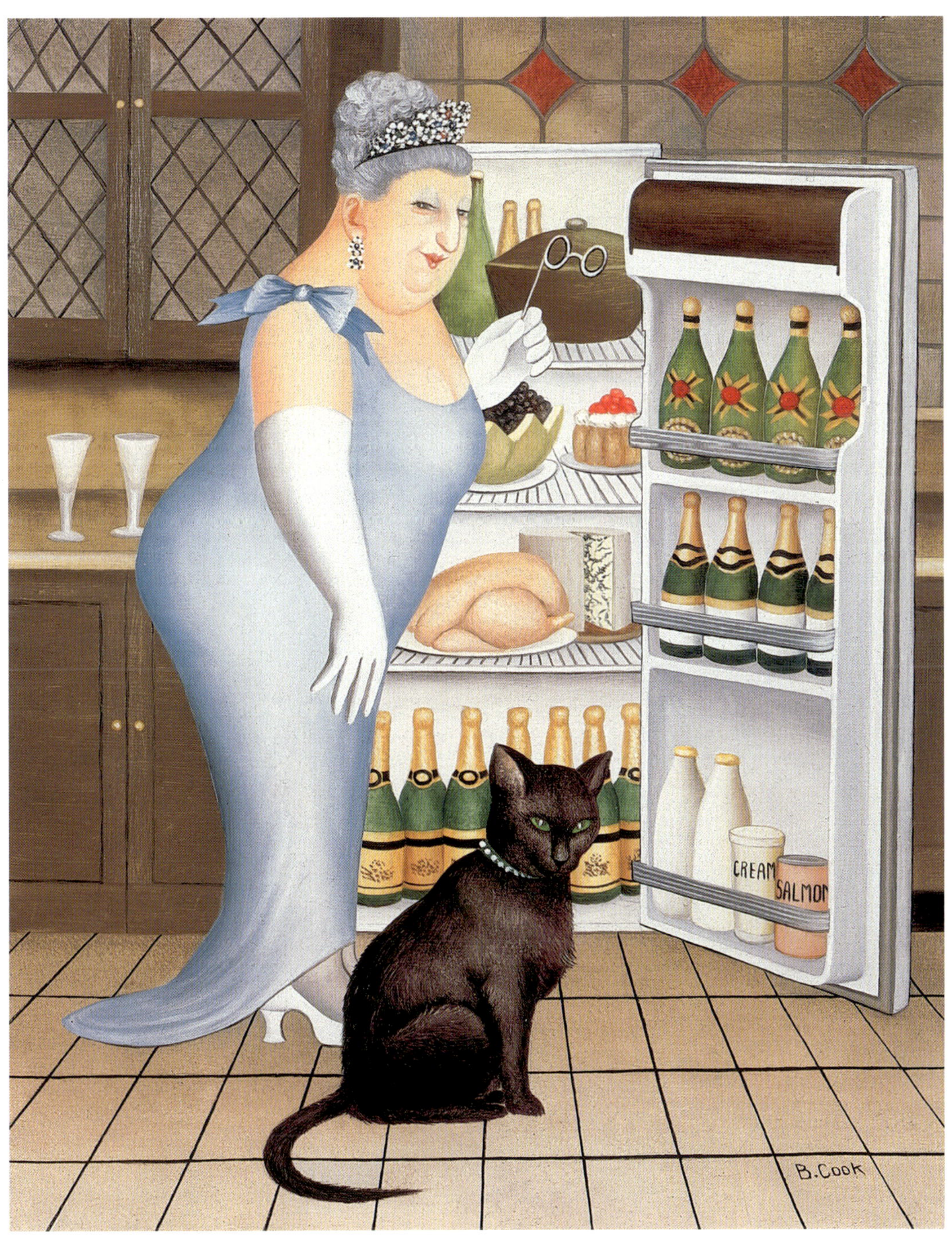

Percy at the Fridge
1989

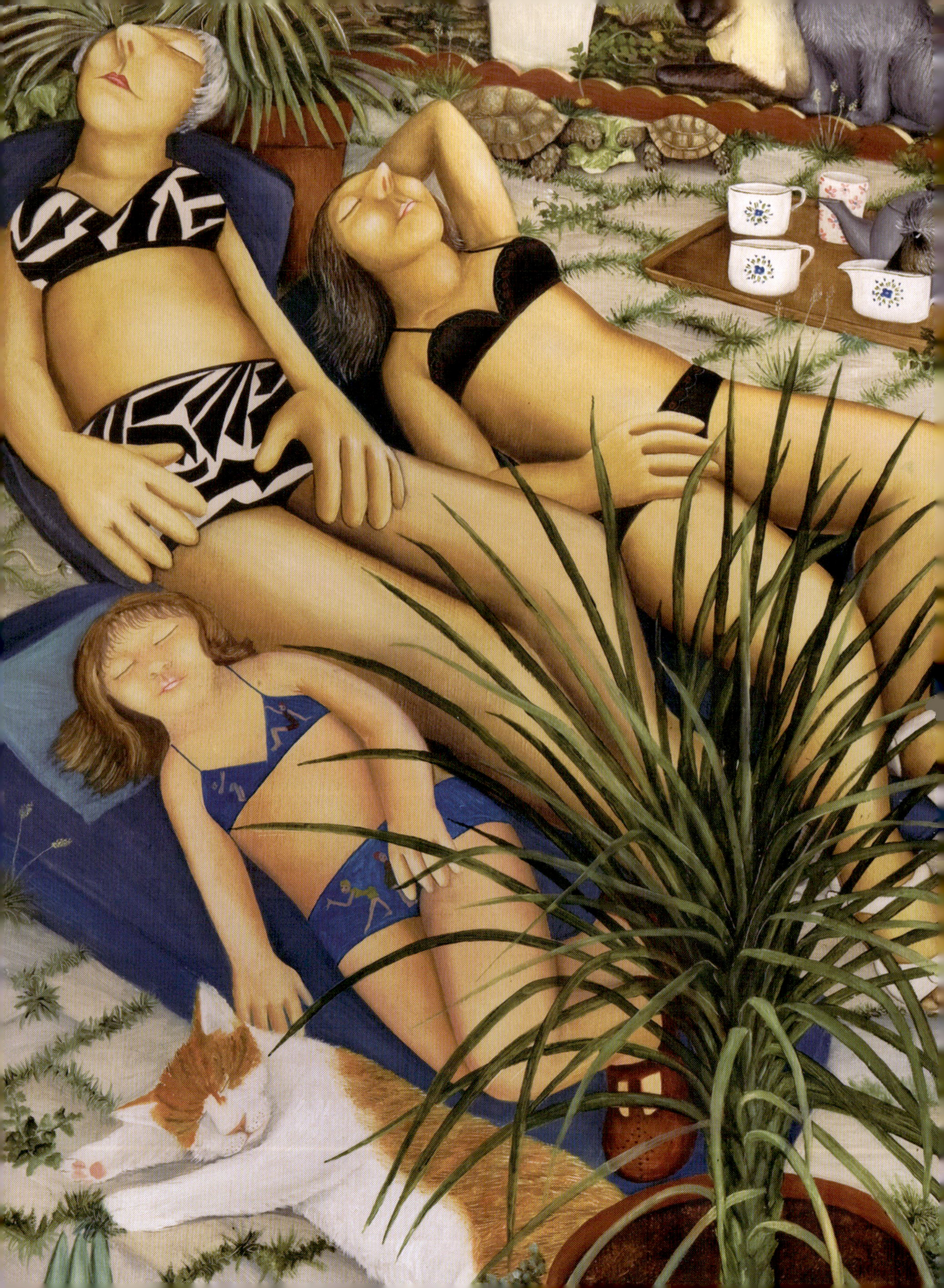

Setting the Scene

Bernard Samuels

I first met Beryl Cook in the spring of 1975. Later that year I presented an exhibition of her work at Plymouth Arts Centre where I had been Director since 1971. It was the first ever showing of her work in a gallery. Thirty years on from then I have recounted the story many times: how I heard about Beryl Cook from an actor on tour in Plymouth who was lodging with Mrs. Cook; how it took me weeks to persuade her to let me put on an exhibition, but strictly on condition, laid down by Mrs Cook, that there would be no publicity; how I broke my promise and telephoned *The Sunday Times* who published a feature article, including a front page cover in February 1976 which made her world famous in a day which ended with a telephone call to my flat in Plymouth Arts Centre from Lionel Levy of the Portal Gallery, the gallery who have shown the work ever since.

Naturally, I have extremely vivid memories of first meeting Beryl Cook and her family – who must always be emphasized as they were so central to her life. My memories are key to my contribution to this book. However, this publication is also a good opportunity to go back and take a look at Plymouth as a context for the extraordinary phenomenon of Beryl Cook's first exhibition.

Like Beryl, I am not a local person. She and her family came to live in Plymouth in 1968. I came to Plymouth in 1956 to teach French at Plymouth College, the local direct grant grammar school. I grew up in Manchester in the 1940s where, in spite of the war, it was possible to enjoy a rich cultural life. Plymouth was still very much a city recovering from the Blitz and cultural life was scarcely on the agenda. Significant change at the civic level was extremely slow in coming. It came eventually in 1982, over 40 years after the Blitz, with the opening of the Theatre Royal.

The long delay did not do many favours for the reputation of the city. The general perception was of a working class town where there was very little money, its life dominated by the naval dockyard and Nonconformism. To a large extent this was an accurate impression, but, in my opinion, by no means the entire picture. There was another side to the coin, one to which I think one can relate the near volcanic force with which Beryl Cook emerged on the arts scene, nationally and internationally, to the chagrin perhaps of some in the art world, but not for the huge numbers of people from many different backgrounds who responded at the time of her first exhibition and for years thereafter.

For thousands who spent time in the services during and after World War II, Plymouth was and still is remembered for Union Street, a straight and, unusually for Plymouth, absolutely flat artery, consisting from one end to the other of shops, including a number of menswear outlets catering for the services; pubs, some small, some enormous; cafés, mainly of the greasy spoon kind providing breakfast for people, local or otherwise, who frequented the area; at least one antique dealer trading at the top end of the market, and one landmark building, the Palace Theatre, a fine Victorian theatre at that time mostly presenting what might best be called shows for the troops, little else. There was also a fair degree of living accommodation above the various premises.

One has to have some conception of Union Street to have some idea of the feel of the town. Built in prosperous Georgian times to link Plymouth and Devonport, by the end of the nineteenth century its stylishness had faded and eventually it became known round the world in the naval fraternity for it whores. Though now an untidy extension of Royal Parade, the city centre's main street, with less than a 100 yard stretch of the original buildings still left, in the minds of many local people it is still a place of shame and focus at weekends for drunkenness. Others, with a feeling for its past, right up until the immediate post-world war decades, might see it as a reflection of the more rumbustious side of the town's vitality.

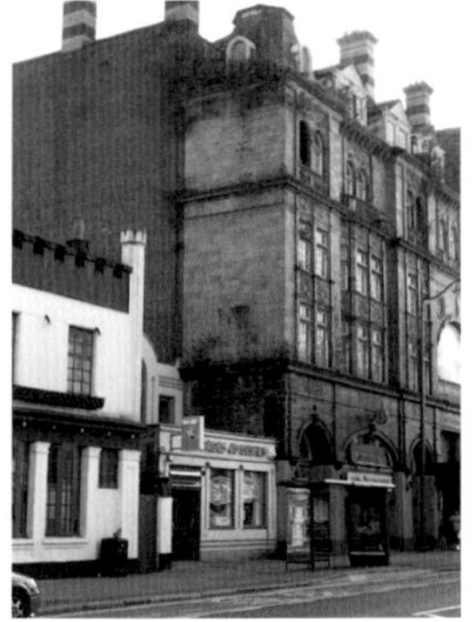

Fig. 8 Union Street buildings, 2008

As well as having Union Street to give character and distinction of a certain kind to the town, the city did not lack for exceptional individuals and enterprises.

I wonder how many people in the town are aware now of the fact that in the 1960s, through to the early 1970s, Plymouth was home to one of the most vibrant rock venues in the country. It was called the Van Dike Club, with premises in Devonport, not far from Aggie Weston's Sailor's Rest Home. The business belonged to the Van Dike family. Night in night out, seven nights a week, in a venue holding just a few hundred people, the club presented famous groups from round the world. The Pink Floyd was just one of many.

Likewise in terms of youth culture, Plymouth, always considered to be at the end of the line, did not miss out on the 1960s vogue of the coffee bar; El Sombrero, located in the area of the city centre, stands out most clearly in my memory. It has long since disappeared, swallowed up in the 1960s in the original Drake Circus development, itself demolished and replaced only recently as a sparkling new shopping mall.

At the same time Devonport Guildhall – which dates from the time of the Napoleonic wars and looks with monumental grandeur down Ker Street – was home for some years during the 1960s and early 1970s to one of the best folk clubs in the country. This was entirely due to Cyril Tawney, a Hampshire man who joined the navy at 16 and later became a well-known figure nationally as a leading force in the folk revival that began in the 1950s.

Rock and folk music were certainly alive and kicking in Plymouth. Perhaps most extraordinary for a town so often dubbed a cultural desert, Plymouth in the early 1960s was home to some of the most brilliant British jazz musicians of their time: Mike Westbrook, John Surman and Keith Rowe. Mike Westbrook and Keith Rowe were students at Plymouth College of Art. They were much influenced by hearing some of the greats of Modern Jazz who arrived in Plymouth in the 1950s, still in the US Navy, found their way to Union Street and performed there. Another astonishing, little-known fact of life in post war Plymouth! By the later years of the 1960s, Westbrook, Surman and Rowe, had become established names in European avant-garde jazz. However, before they left, mainly to play on the European circuit, it was possible to hear them in never-to-be-forgotten concerts in the city as they reached their peak.

In the field of literature, Charles Causley, though quintessentially a Cornishman with his home in Launceston, had close ties with the city through his years serving in the Navy. He took part in readings in the town, appearing memorably on one occasion under the aegis of Plymouth Arts Centre on the same platform as Cyril Tawney: he was the nearest the city had to a resident poet. In prose, though I'm prepared to stand corrected, the city has yet to produce a writer of note. The most interesting writer living in the town, at the time in question, was the novelist Philip Callow who had somehow found his way from Nottingham, a writer in fact very much in the tradition of D H Lawrence.

If the written word seems under-represented in Plymouth, the story is very different for the visual arts. The city has a significant place in the history of British art that takes in Joshua Reynolds, who was born in Plympton (1723), Benjamin Haydon who was born in Plymouth (1786), Charles Eastlake, born in Plymouth (1793), pupil of Haydon and first director of the National Gallery, and J M W Turner who, as a celebrated visiting artist, memorably recorded landscape views of the city including his famous painting of Devonport Dockyard from Mount Edgcumbe.

Leaping forward to Plymouth after World War II one finds no shortage of painters, traditional and modern. Plymouth is, in a sense, the gateway to Cornwall. Some people might say it is where Cornwall begins! It is certainly the case that many people, drawn to spend time in the region by the attractions of Cornwall, saw Plymouth as a stopping off point, got this far and decided to put down roots here or on the banks of the Tamar River. In fact there is a strong case to be made for the richness of the visual arts scene in Plymouth in the post war era.

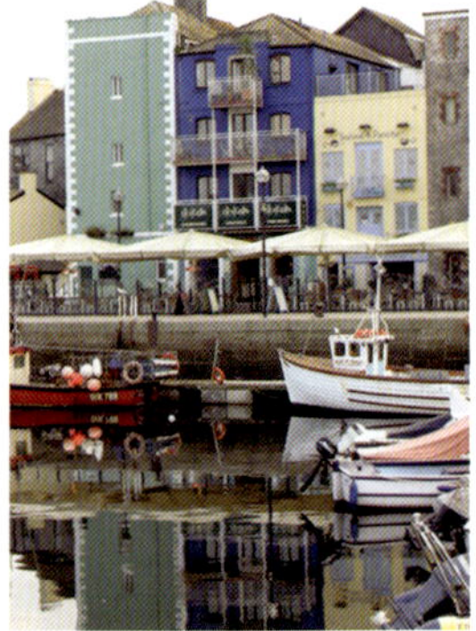

Fig. 9 Barbican 2008

The city's Barbican area and its warehouses (plus allied watering holes) provided a natural environment for artists, many of them former students of Plymouth College of Art. One such example is Vincent Bennett. A Plymothian born and bred, he was at a brief stage in his life, a boxer. A man of wry, sardonic humour, his creative imagination fired by his passion for American cinema, he recycled his native experience of the city into his brilliantly colourful and often outrageously comic paintings.

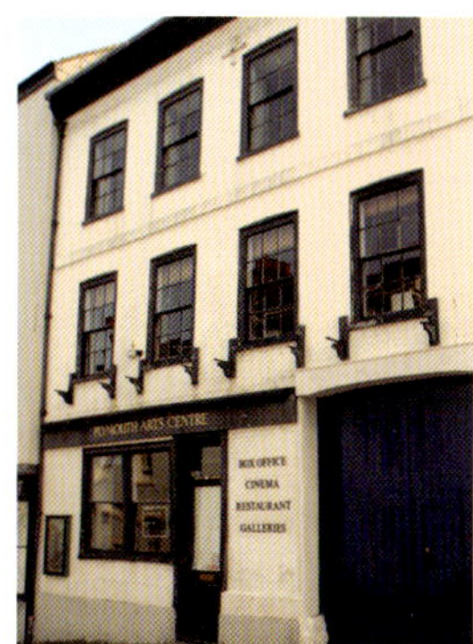

Fig. 10 Plymouth Arts Centre 2008

The range of activities was diverse. For instance, the 1960s also saw the arrival in Plymouth of Robert Lenkiewicz, an artist with a very different agenda. The murals he painted in the Barbican, based on his interest in esoteric writers and philosophers of the Elizabethan period, incorporated numerous local people, the whole enterprise going completely counter to the artistic orthodoxies of the day.

I have by no means covered all that I recall from this period. I have simply homed in on some distinctive elements of life, art, the world of entertainment – call it what you will – in Plymouth at the time when Beryl Cook and her husband John moved here; 'lively goings on', you might call them, which gave the city, regardless of official attitudes, a vitality, a quality which was always of paramount importance to the Cooks.

§

And so to the Plymouth Arts Centre which played such an important role in the launch of the career of Beryl Cook.

Plymouth Arts Centre grew out of the importance during and after World War II of the government's programme of arts and educational activities for the services. It found a home in Virginia House, a Social Settlement, created by Lady Nancy Astor in the Barbican in the late 1920s during her years as Member of Parliament for Plymouth Sutton. Technically the Centre was a private club with a few rooms within a wing of the Settlement which housed various members of the Settlement staff, dedicated to helping the numerous families in the chronically deprived neighbourhood that the Barbican was then.

In practice the Arts Centre was a haven during the years immediately after the war for local people and others whose lives for all kind of reasons, work, family, had brought them to Plymouth and who were keenly interested in the arts. The facilities were extremely limited, to put it mildly, but not its cultural horizons. Mike Westbrook, John Surman and friends used the basement of the Looe Street building for rehearsals. The minute theatre space presented theatre of the most adventurous kind of its day, performed by locally based amateurs and professionals. The first play I saw not long after I arrived in Plymouth was an excellent production of Jean Genêt's 'The Maids' in the Arts Centre, at that time something you might perhaps expect to come across in the Arts Theatre in London, hardly in Plymouth, home to dockyardies and Methodism.

Plymouth Arts Centre was set up in the late 1940s. However by the late 1950s/ early 1960s it had begun to lose some of its initial impetus. By then the burning issue for the arts in the city was the serious lack of arts provision: no proper theatre suitable for a city of quarter of a million, no proper concert hall, no provision for cinema other than commercial cinema, and precious little space apart from the City Art Gallery to show new work in the visual arts.

Like scores of other people in the city, I joined the campaign to remedy these major gaps. However, in the course of all this campaigning I discovered that Plymouth Arts Centre, through the initiative of Bob Myers, a Yorkshireman and a newcomer to the area, had begun to promote a series of chamber music concerts of the highest quality. These were presented by the Centre in the 352 seat Athenaeum Theatre. For me they were the life-blood of classical music in the city.

I began to take an interest in the Arts Centre as such. This was the 1960s, an extraordinary period of social and cultural change. I began to initiate events in the Centre which tapped into the current trends of the time. Gradually my interest grew to the point where at the end of 1970 I decided to leave teaching and devote my time to working at Plymouth Arts Centre, just myself and a committee, with aspirations to make something of the place. It was certainly a good time to make such a seemingly risky 'career move'. The Centre had no funding to speak of and I had no experience of business or finance, but it was a good moment for someone with a broad interest in the arts, especially if you were keen, as I was, to promote new, contemporary work.

New funding had been created by the government through the Arts Council in the 1960s, the era when Jennie Lee was Minister for the Arts, which immediately made an impact in all art practices. These were exciting times. I saw this as a great opportunity and Plymouth Arts Centre became one of the leading centres in the South West for showing new work. To a great extent the Arts Centre programme was based on touring professional actors and musicians with support from the Arts Council. It is against this background, one could say ferment, given the intensity of the programme, that I came to meet Beryl Cook.

Whilst the Arts Centre was a focus for new work on the national level, it certainly had a local mission. Every arts centre director dreams, I suppose, that one day an artist of exceptional talent will be found on the doorstep. Certainly, whilst promoting numerous artists of all kinds who of necessity toured nationally, I think I always had one eye open and one ear cocked for someone or something extraordinary to appear near to hand. Beryl Cook, so fate would have it, lived 10 minutes walk away from Plymouth Arts Centre.

§

My chief recollection of Beryl from my first meetings with her was of her great uncertainty. "Perhaps you could organize an exhibition for the residents in an old people's home" was one of the first ideas that Beryl put to me. In spite of all the hesitancy what did come through was the fact that I was dealing with someone who was passionate in her interest in art, entirely self-taught maybe, but with a very keen grasp of the work of artists she admired, in particular Stanley Spencer and the more recherché figure of Edward Burra, as well as various eccentric self-taught artists.

The final breakthrough came – I think it was during our third or fourth meeting – when I came up with the suggestion that I put on an exhibition in the Arts Centre that would include all the work she had so far produced, i.e. all the work in the house plus the work belonging to Tony Martin, an antique dealer friend in Looe who had in fact sold some of her work from his shop.

The exhibition opened in November 1975. I saw a good deal of Beryl before and after the exhibition. My memories of what we talked about at first and on the many occasions we met later are difficult to unravel. But it is impossible to forget the massive response to her exhibition. It would be dishonest to suggest that I knew in advance that the response would be on such a scale. The excitement, the letters and messages from many parts of the world, continued a very long time; I think it took several years to abate. At the same time Beryl became, in a sense, part of the story of Plymouth Arts Centre.

Putting my recollections in some kind of order, the enthusiasm of John and Beryl for the pubs in Union Street was something I became aware of very early on. Their favourite haunt was The Antelope, a pub one might describe as a pretty basic place, host to some pretty basic folk, the ambience of which stood out in contrast to John and Beryl's agreeable home surroundings, always well kept and tidy even though it was full of Beryl's paintings, dotted around everywhere, on the walls, along the skirtingboards, amid her numerous favourite *objets d'art* reflecting her love of Art Deco.

Once the exhibition had been agreed on and the initial response had been encouraging, I began joining them for drinks in pubs they frequented here and there in the town, places where they would be greeted by the regulars, very frequently gay men and women who seemed to look on Beryl as a favourite friend, and in some way a protector. This was perhaps not surprising given the extent to which some of these people featured in her work. However, the time was the mid-1970s and the gay community was still very much seen as aberrant.

This association seemed to blossom forth in the wake of the success of the first show. The splendid front cover of the now famous February 1976 article in *The Sunday Times* which played such a vital role in launching the career of Beryl Cook shows the ground floor bar of the Lockyer Hotel, at that time the last remaining old style, somewhat seedy, commercial hotel in the city centre, now long gone in the redevelopment around the bomb site from which grew the present day Theatre Royal. The foreground of the picture is dominated by the sturdy arm of a buxom, blonde barmaid, on the left in the background a gay male couple who were a regular feature of the establishment. That same bar could from time to time be turned into the performance space for shows devised by the gay men who frequented the place, outrageous extravaganzas designed by Brian Pearce, at one time a window dresser at Harrods, later a professional club performer, who appeared in his full exuberance in several post-first exhibition paintings. The shows seemed to chime in with some of the wildly way-out work that was presented in the less than basic facility that was the ground floor performance space in Plymouth Arts Centre, later smartened up – under my watch, I must confess – into a gallery/foyer leading into the present cinema which was created in the 1980s.

The reaction to Beryl's first exhibition, which contained everything from her roughest, first efforts through to fully fledged paintings such as the soon-to-be-celebrated 'Sabotage' and 'Five Hungry Cats', was instantaneous. The word seemed to spread like wildfire and in no time my promise of "no publicity" had gone by the wayside.

From then on, certainly for the next few years, the career of Beryl Cook had something of the feel of a non-stop circus show with something new happening all the time. The February 1976 article in *The Sunday Times* colour supplement was quickly followed by the first exhibition at the Portal Gallery. The event that stands out in my memory was the review by the well known critic Edward Lucie-Smith on 'Kaleidoscope', Radio Four's regular midweek evening arts slot just before the Ten O'Clock News. In no time Beryl had moved from unknown Plymouth landlady to nationally talked of artist-to-be-watched. Edward (he soon became a close friend of John's and Beryl's) was already a highly regarded writer on art and a sophisticated commentator on the arts scene of the day with a distinct touch of the maverick. He made a particularly perceptive comment on the way the accidental distortions in the early paintings worked to their advantage and were in fact part of their strength.

Shortly afterwards the Arts Centre was contacted by the Whitechapel Gallery, the famous gallery in the East End with strong links to that community, a venue which I held in high esteem. I went up to London to meet with the administration of the time. The staff had seen the article in *The Sunday Times* and pressed to put on a show as soon as possible. The gallery was between directors. There was a feeling of some urgency on the part of the interim officers who seemed doubtful whether their enthusiasm would get the backing of the incoming director. The exhibition went ahead at relatively short notice. The incoming director, it transpired, was Nicholas Serota, now Director of the Tate and therefore the 'villain of the piece', as it were, in the debate, of which the media are so fond, as to whether the work of Beryl Cook should be included in the Tate Gallery collection, a debate in which Beryl herself took not the slightest interest, finding the whole discussion quite pointless.

And then the ramifications spread abroad. Letters came from round the world, some to Plymouth Arts Centre, some just addressed to “Beryl Cook Plymouth”. Sources of interest were highly diverse. For instance an approach was made by a museum about the butchery trade in Germany. They had seen a painting by Beryl about a butcher’s shop.

Interest in the States came in the form of the directors of the Russian Tearoom, the celebrated New York restaurant, who visited Plymouth to meet Beryl and acquire some paintings.

The demand for publications grew instantly after the first show, leading to visits to Plymouth Arts Centre of leading players in various fields, the Alexander Gallery from Bristol, specialising in limited edition prints, Gallery Five, a leading company publishing greetings cards. I found myself entertaining family directors of John Murray, part of the history of English literature, who were to be the publishers of the first books on Beryl, which in turn led to a very fruitful relationship with Joe Whitlock Blundell, chief executive of the Folio Society, resulting in a number of commissions for illustrated editions of modern literary classics. Beryl Cook, always a keen reader, showed herself to be a brilliantly insightful interpreter, evoking with uncanny accuracy the world of Christopher Isherwood’s *Mr. Norris Changes Trains*, the Edinburgh of Muriel Spark’s *The Prime of Miss Jean Brodie* and Evelyn Waugh’s California in *The Loved One*.

All these business relationships developed into friendships, some of which resulted in fine paintings. Her portrait of Joe Whitlock Blundell is for me one of her finest, a brilliant piece of imaginative characterisation. Of the friendships that grew out of the publicity surrounding the first exhibition, the one she perhaps treasured most was her friendship with the photographer Barbara Ker-Seymer, a close friend of Edward Burra. He saw the article in *The Sunday Times* just before he died and was immediately taken with what he saw, finding in Beryl something of a kindred spirit. Ker-Seymer kindly took the trouble to write and tell her about Burra's reaction. This, one could say, took Beryl into the very heart of the Bohemian world of the inter-war years, a world that had long fascinated her, but one of which her knowledge was second-hand, primarily through books.

Having proved 'a big hit' on her home territory in Plymouth, Beryl's appeal spread among numerous people in the arts, people in publishing, practising artists, restaurateurs whose clientele was very much from the world of the arts, as well as numerous people from the world of the theatre, a whole chapter in themselves. At the time the only professional critic who 'saw the point' immediately was Edward Lucie-Smith. Perhaps we are now seeing a slight shift in the blind resistance of his fellow critics.

To describe my own feeling about Beryl Cook as an artist, I go back to the time of the first exhibition. It seems to me that the great virtue of the work lies in the fact that the heart of it, its central core is located in a particular place, namely Plymouth. The paintings are local through and through, but what is most significant is that they have a quality that enables them to transcend the purely local and gives them an appeal that is completely universal. One knows instinctively that they are saying something truthful about one's fellow human beings in a way that could not be better expressed.

Or, to quote the words of one journalist I spoke to recently: "Beryl struck a chord".

Bernard Samuels was Director of Plymouth Arts Centre, 1971–1996

Location photographs, Sarah Chapman

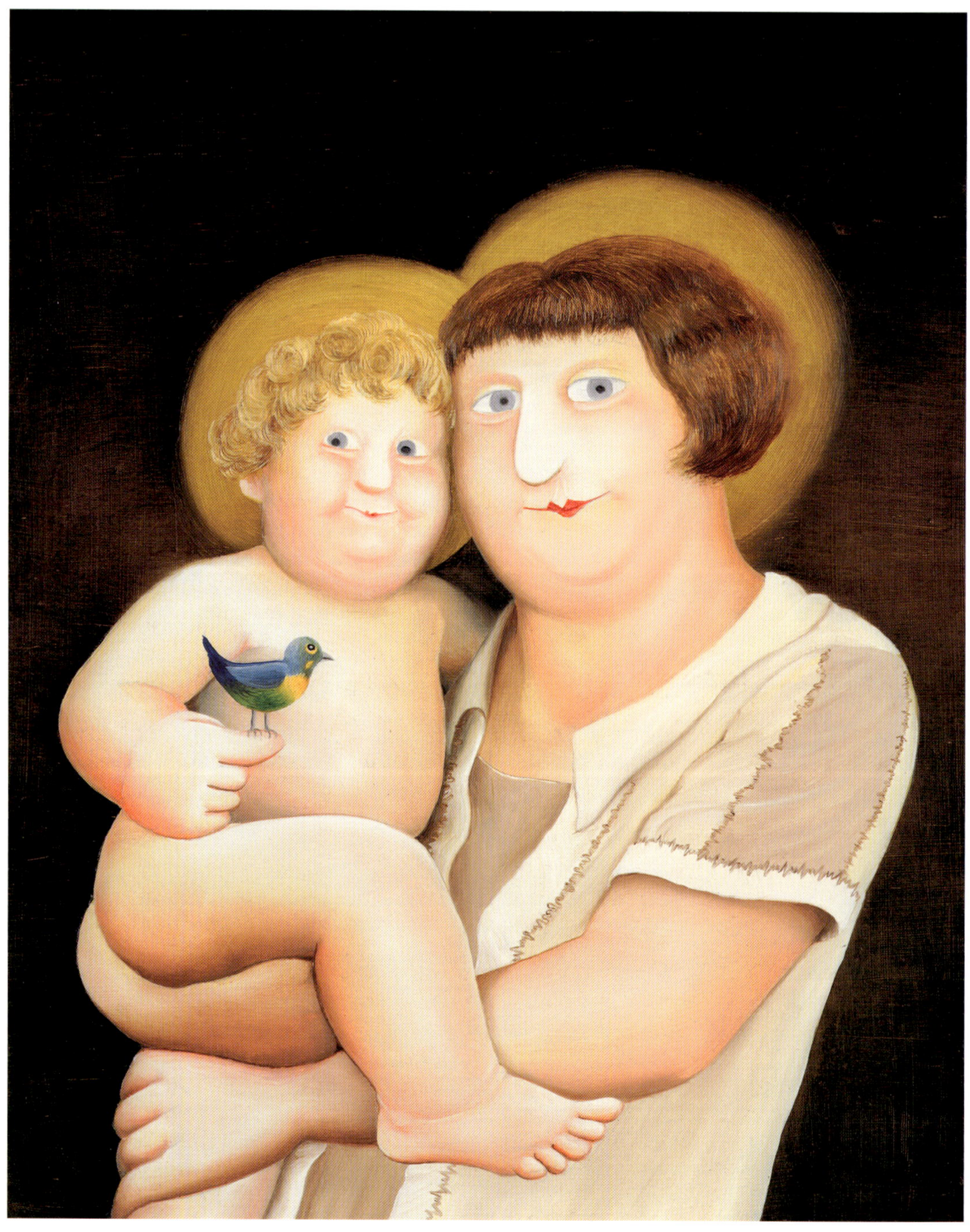

Mother and Child
circa 1980

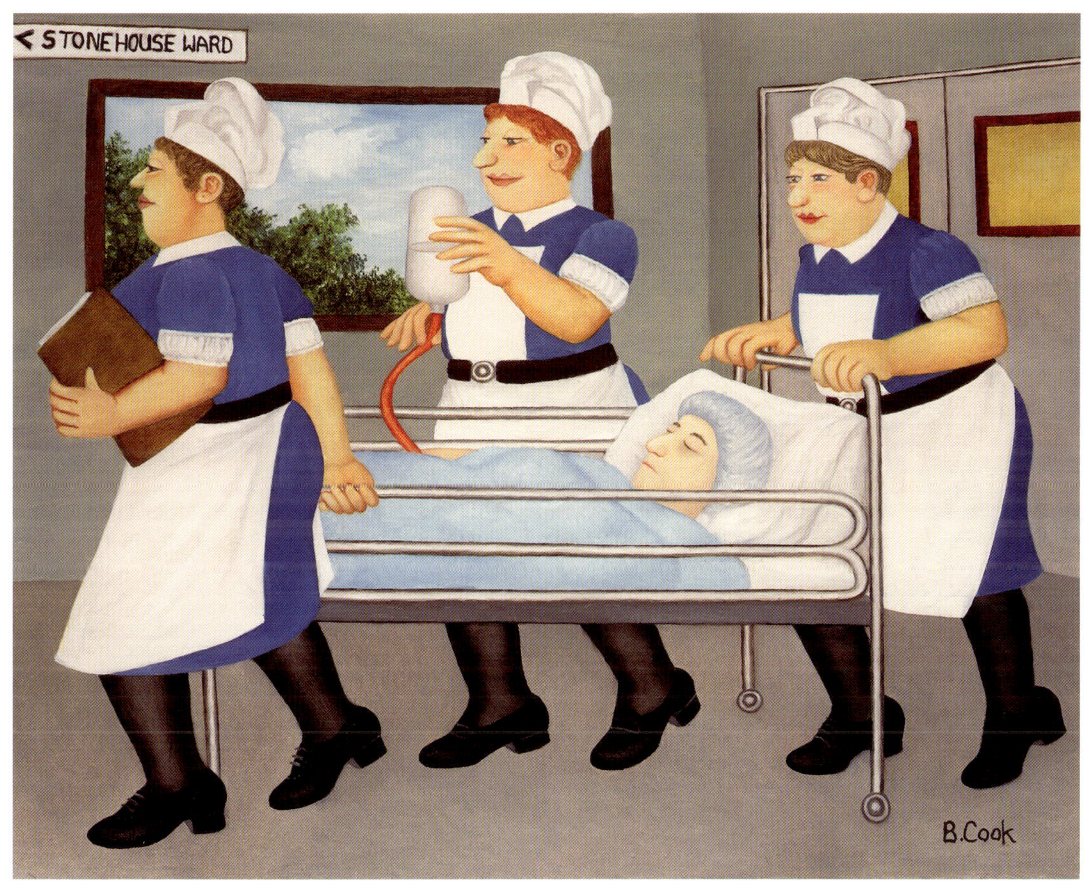

To Stonehouse Ward
2005

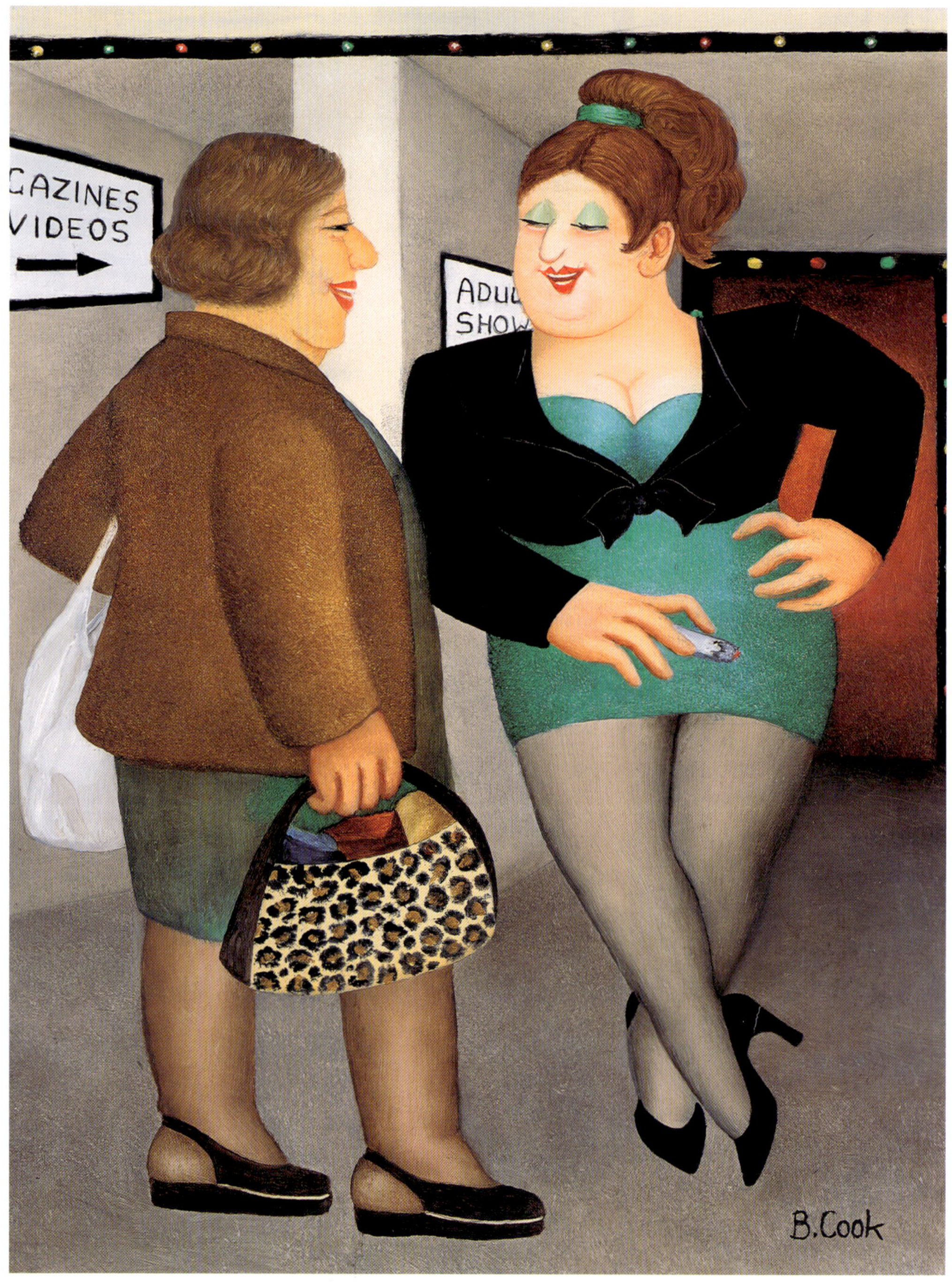

How's Business?
2006

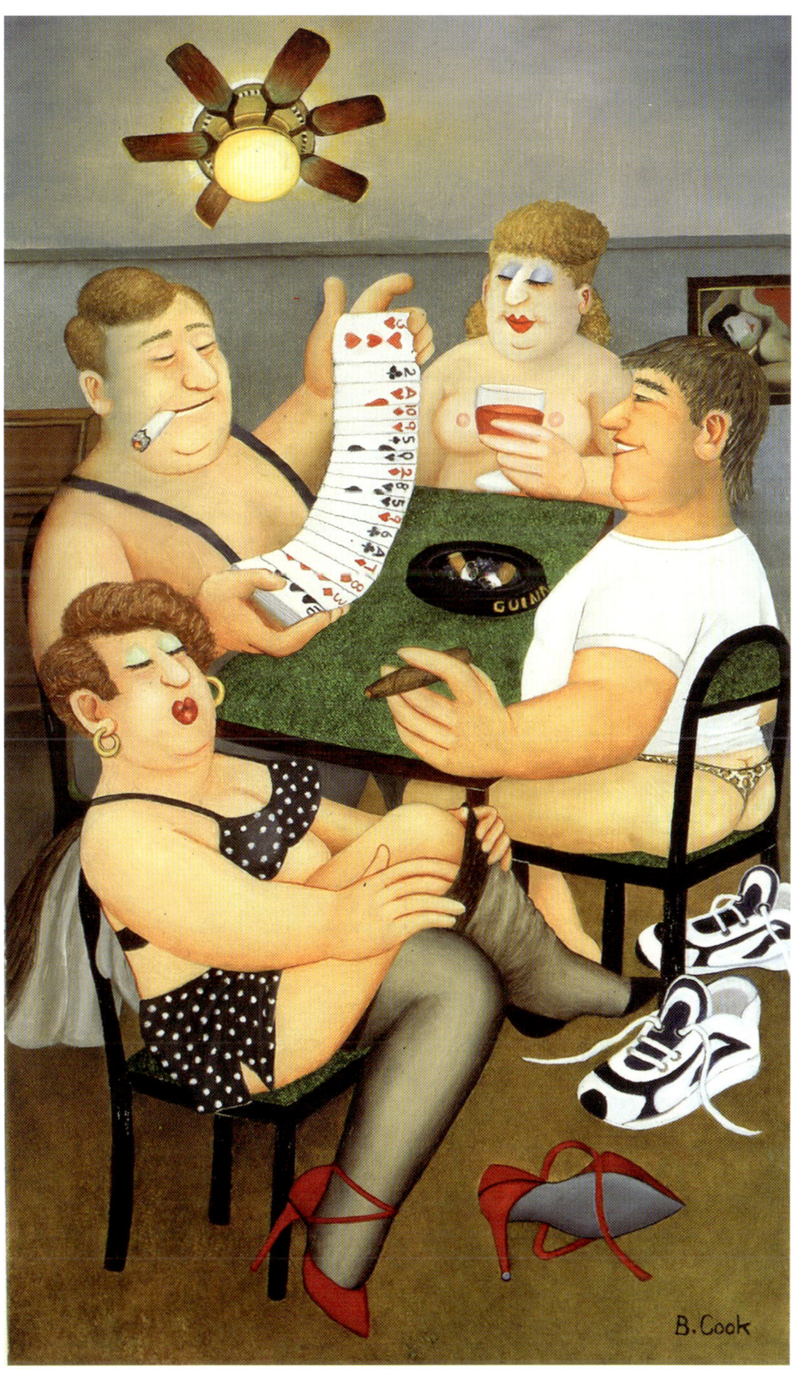

Strip Poker
2006

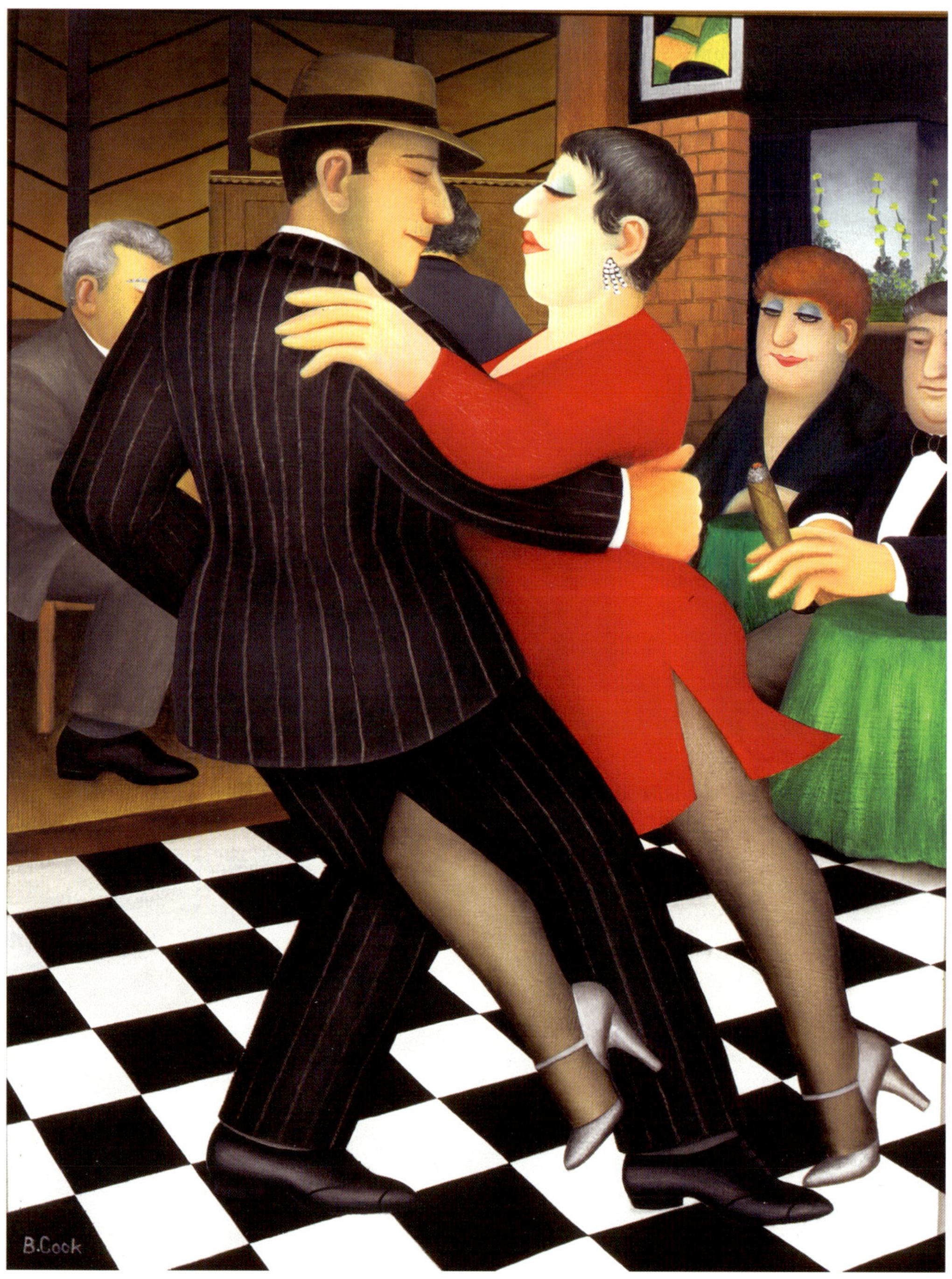

Tango Bar
1994

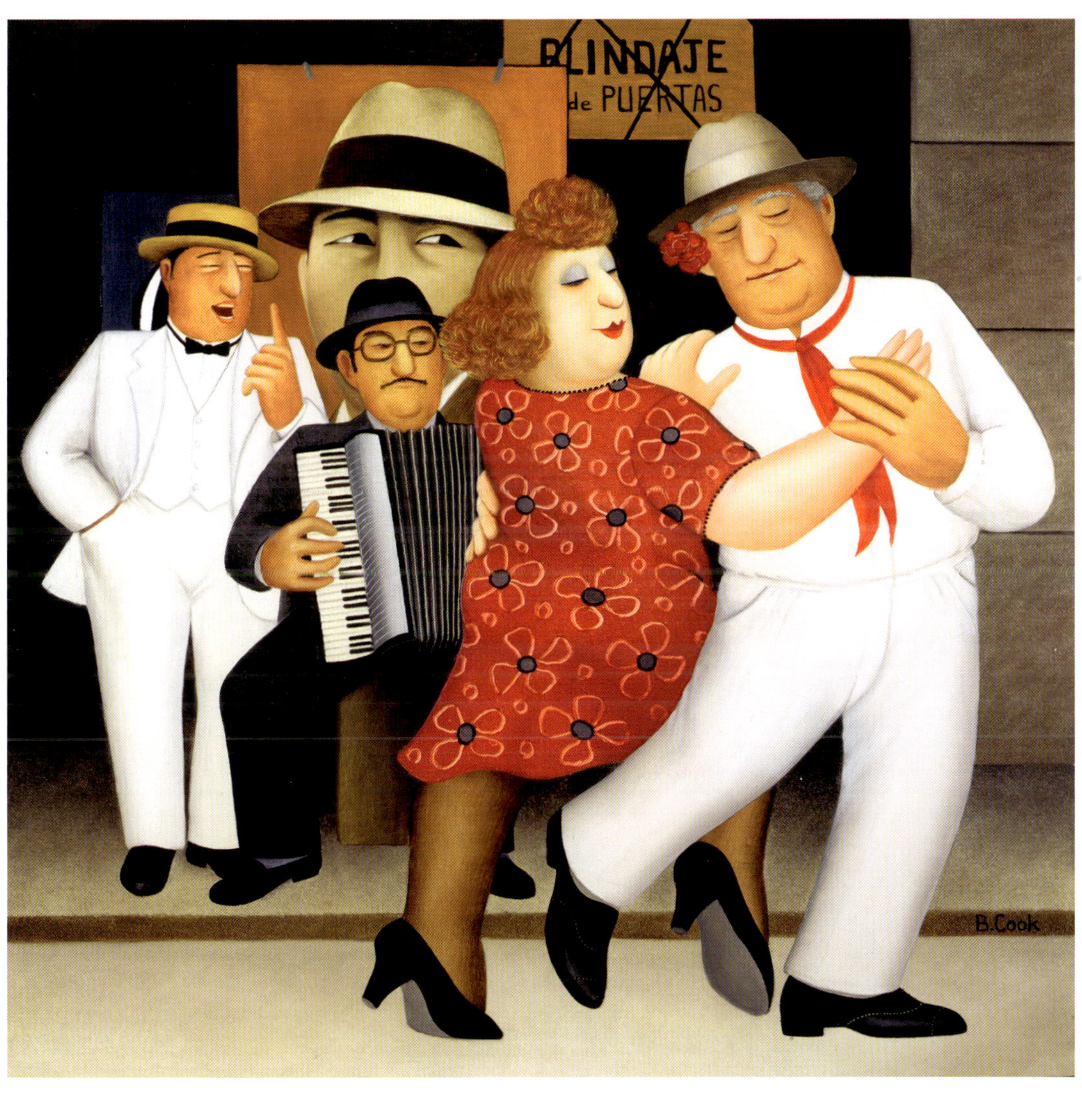

Tango Busking
1995

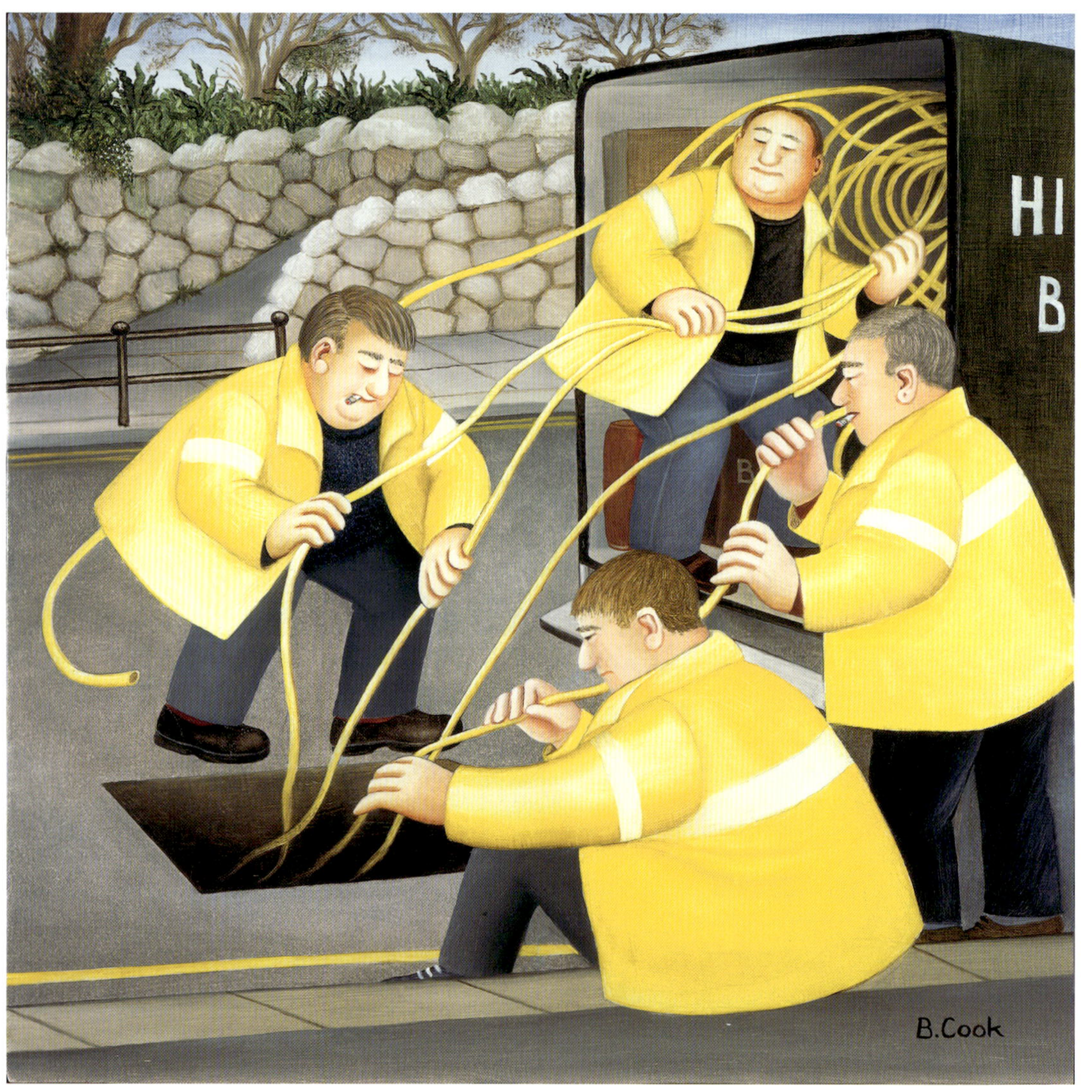

Dyno-Rod
1999

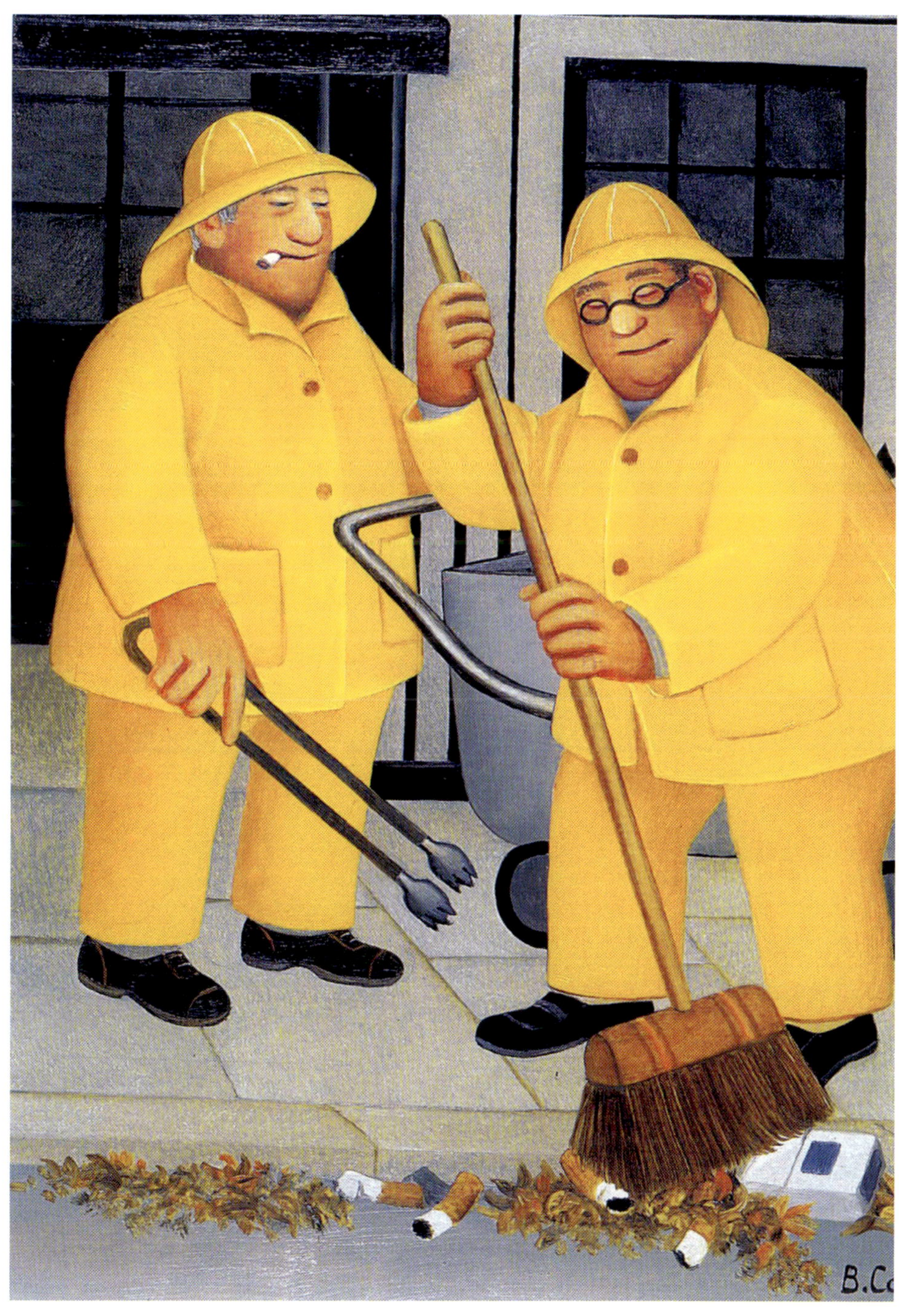

Road Sweepers
1996

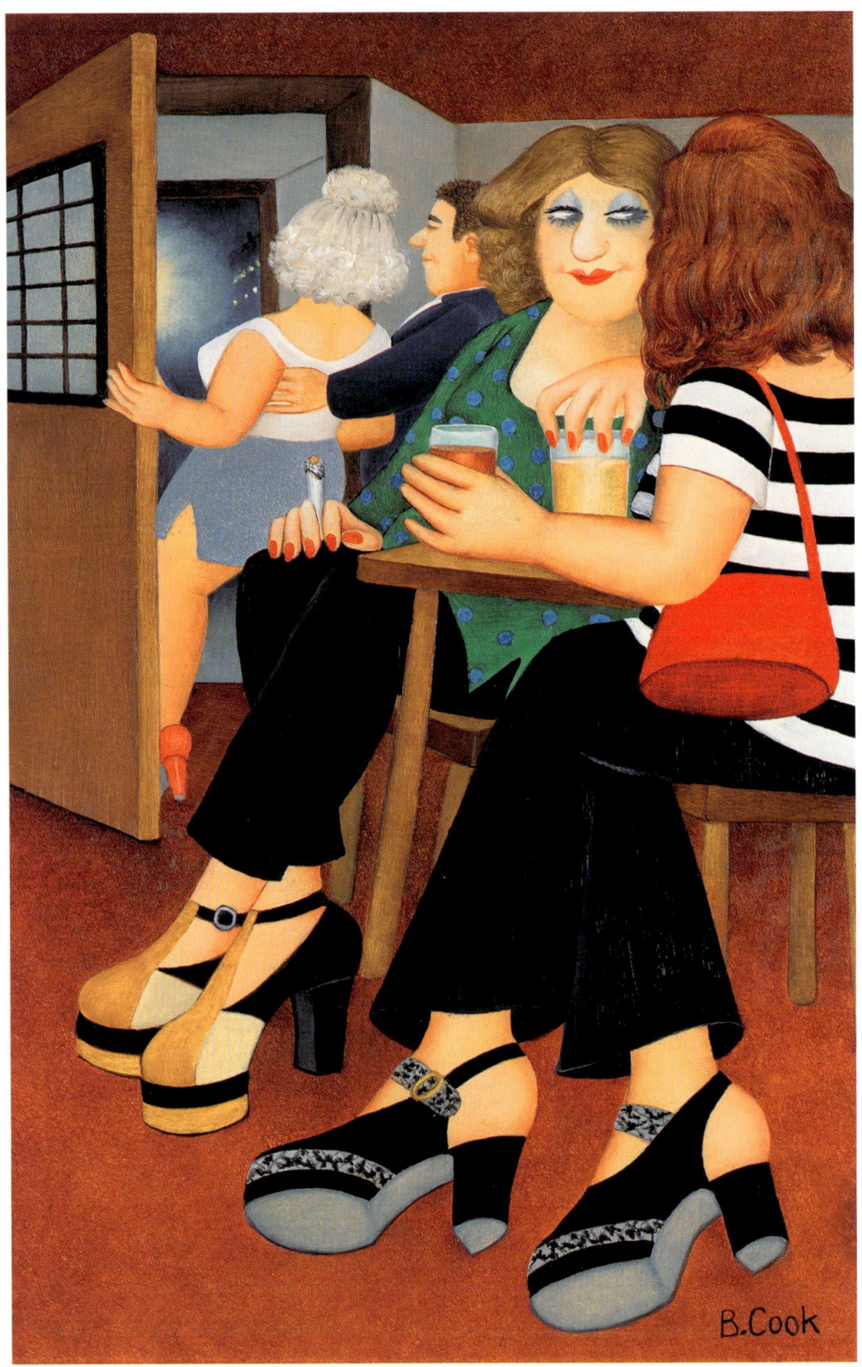

Big Shoes
2006

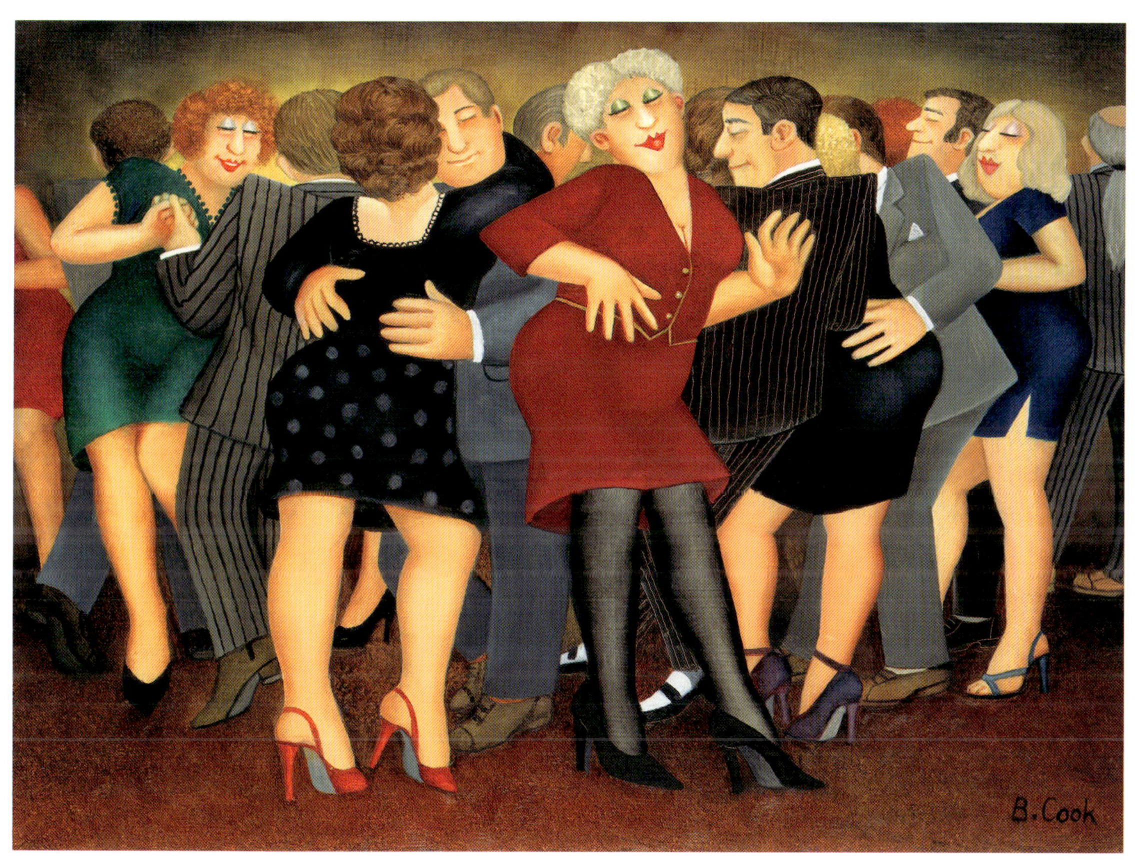

Dancing the Black Bottom
2006

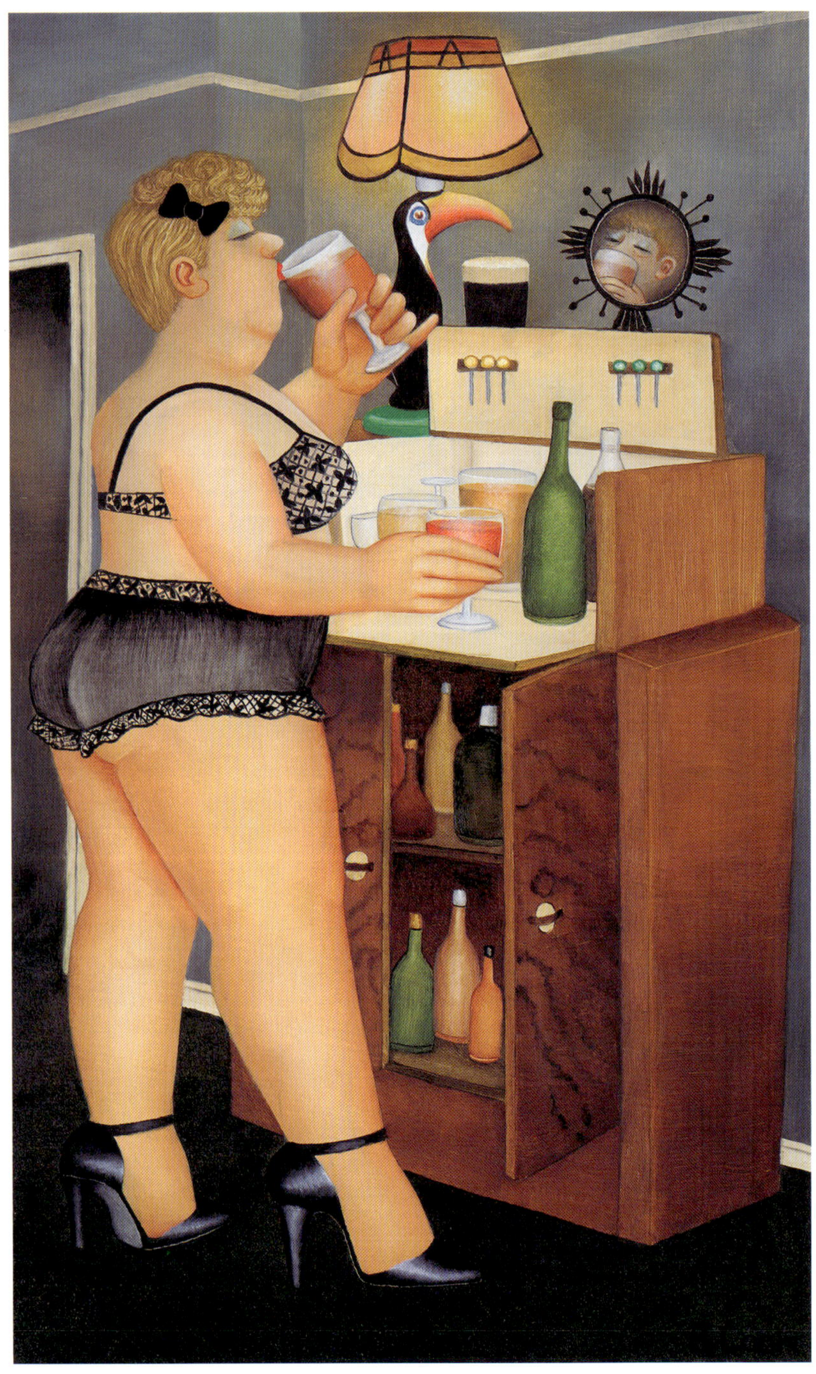

Drinkies
2007

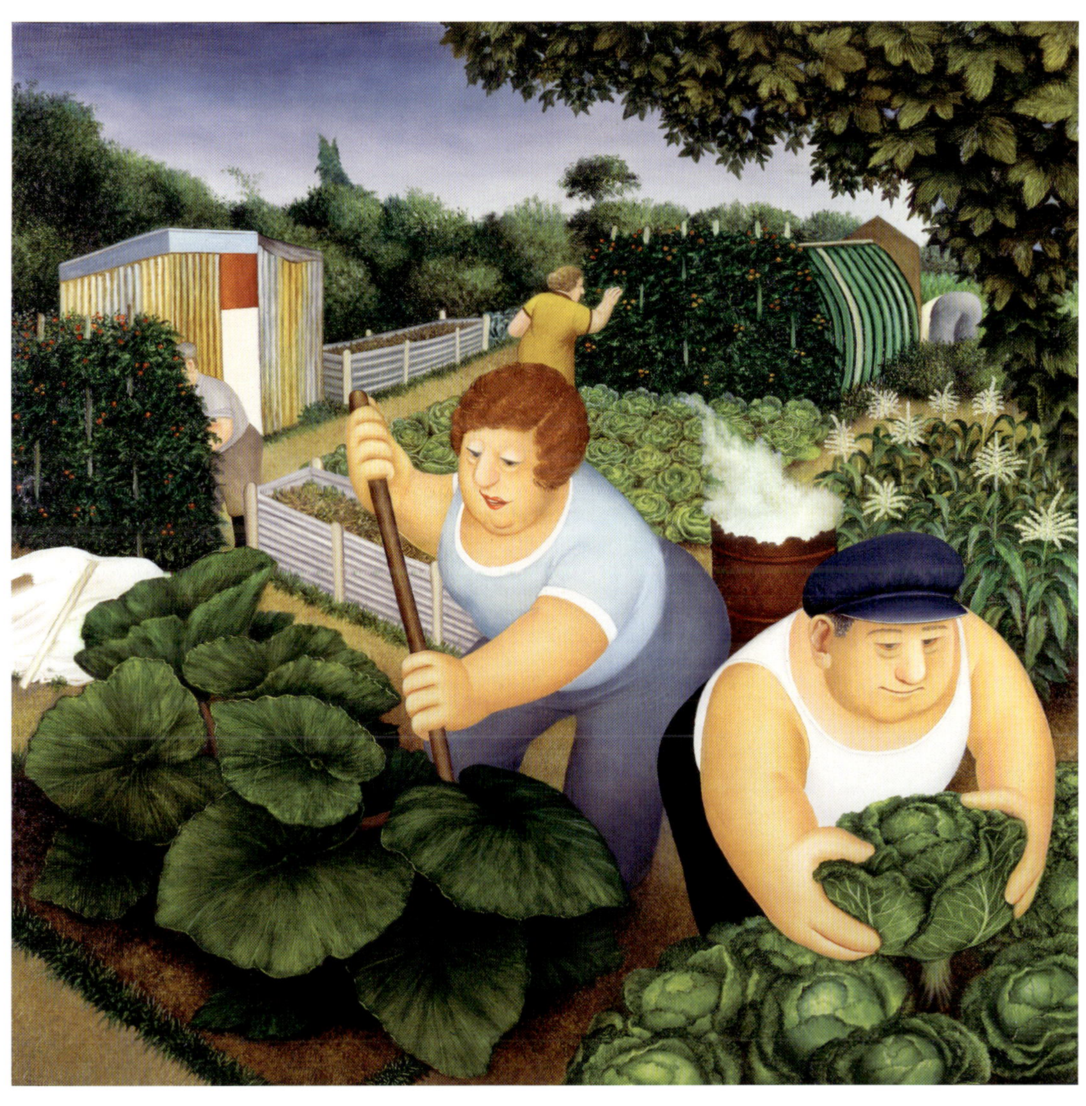

The Allotment
1992

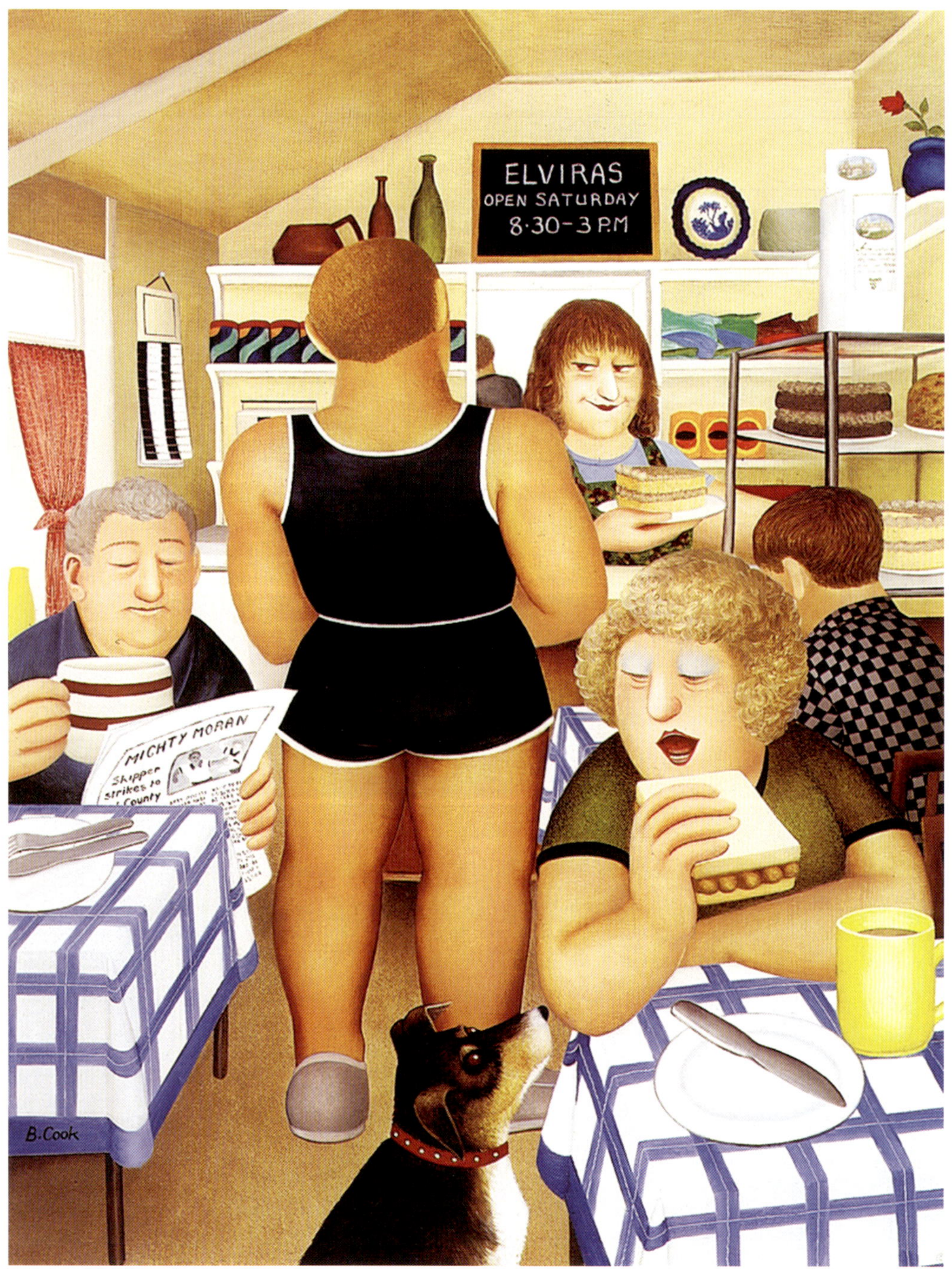

Elvira's Café
1997

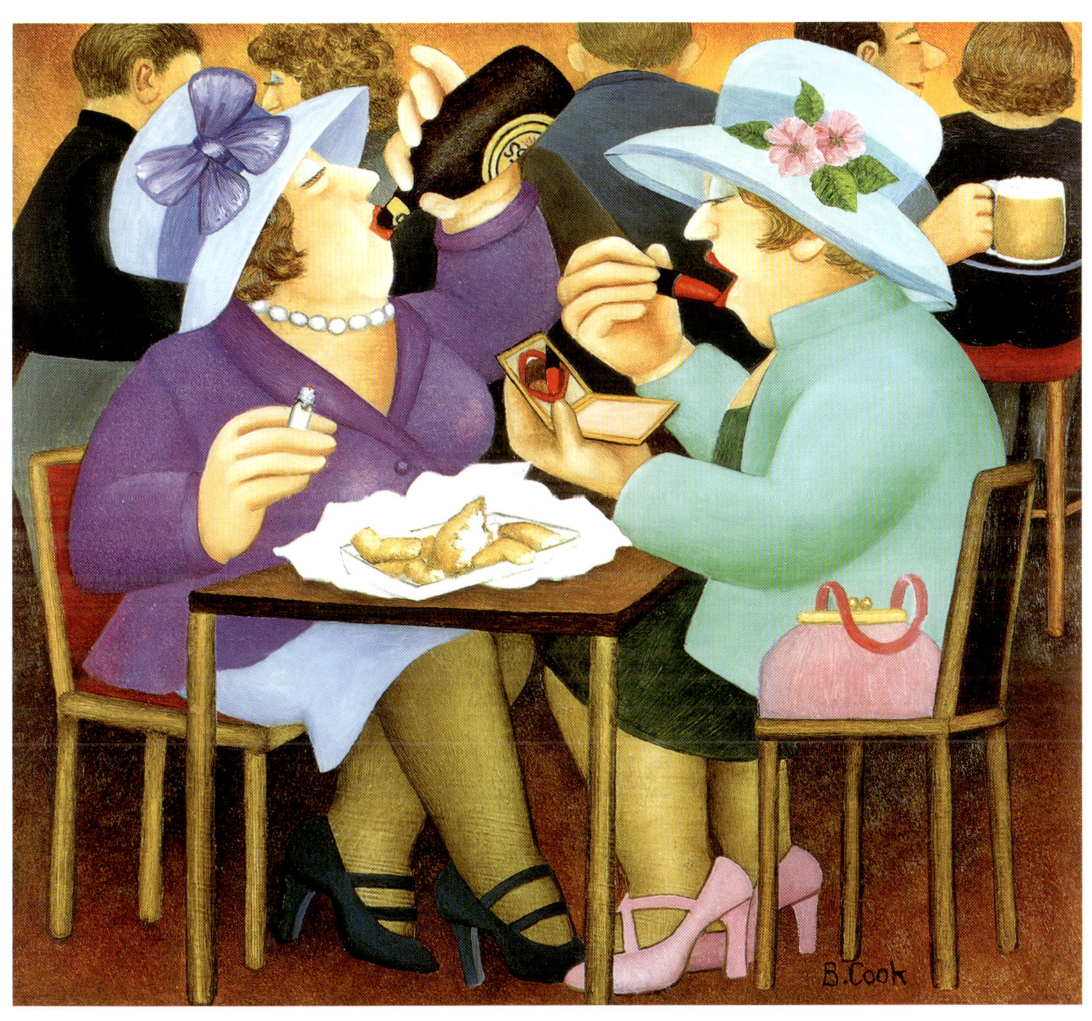

Ladies Doing Lunch
2003

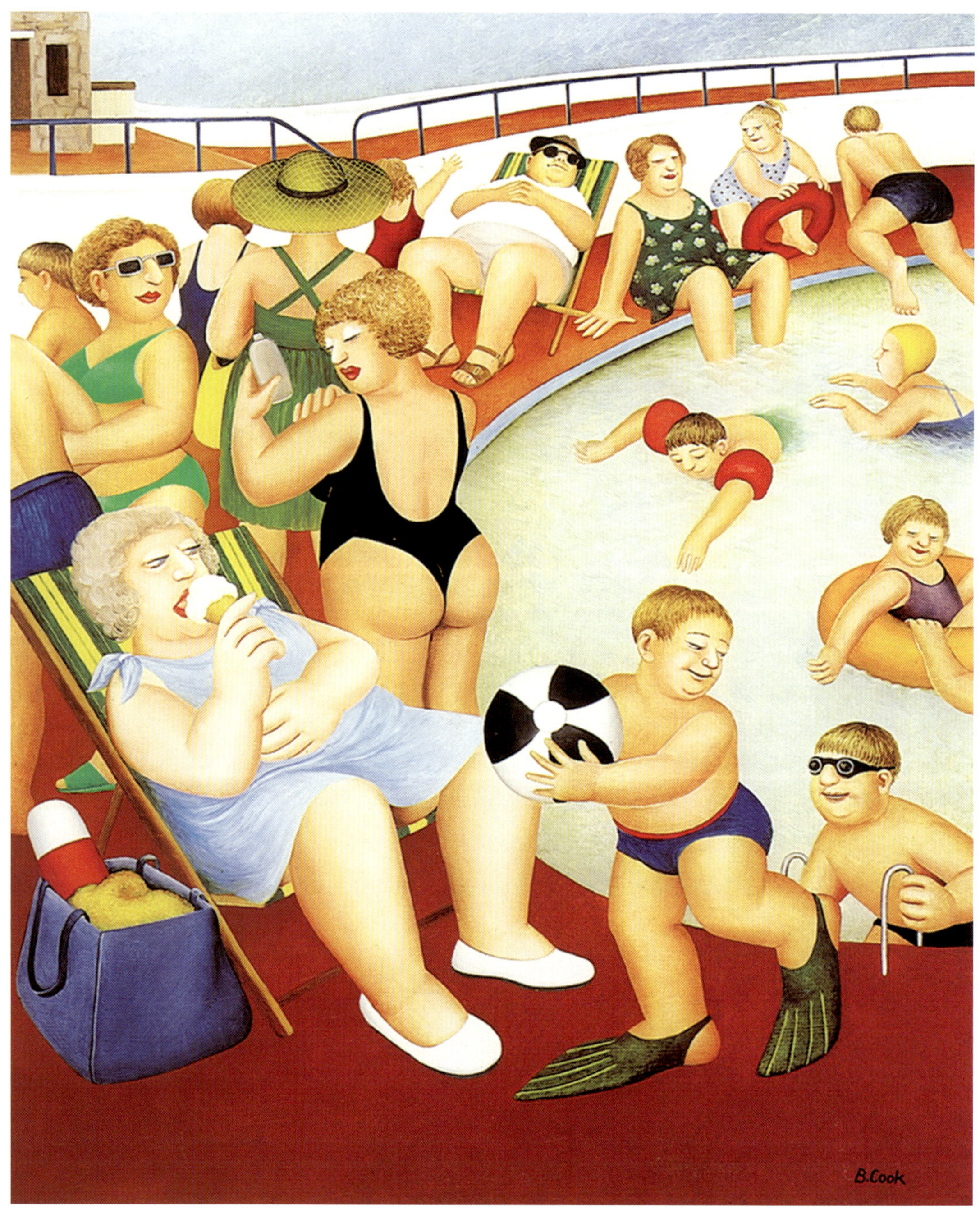

Bathing Pool
1974

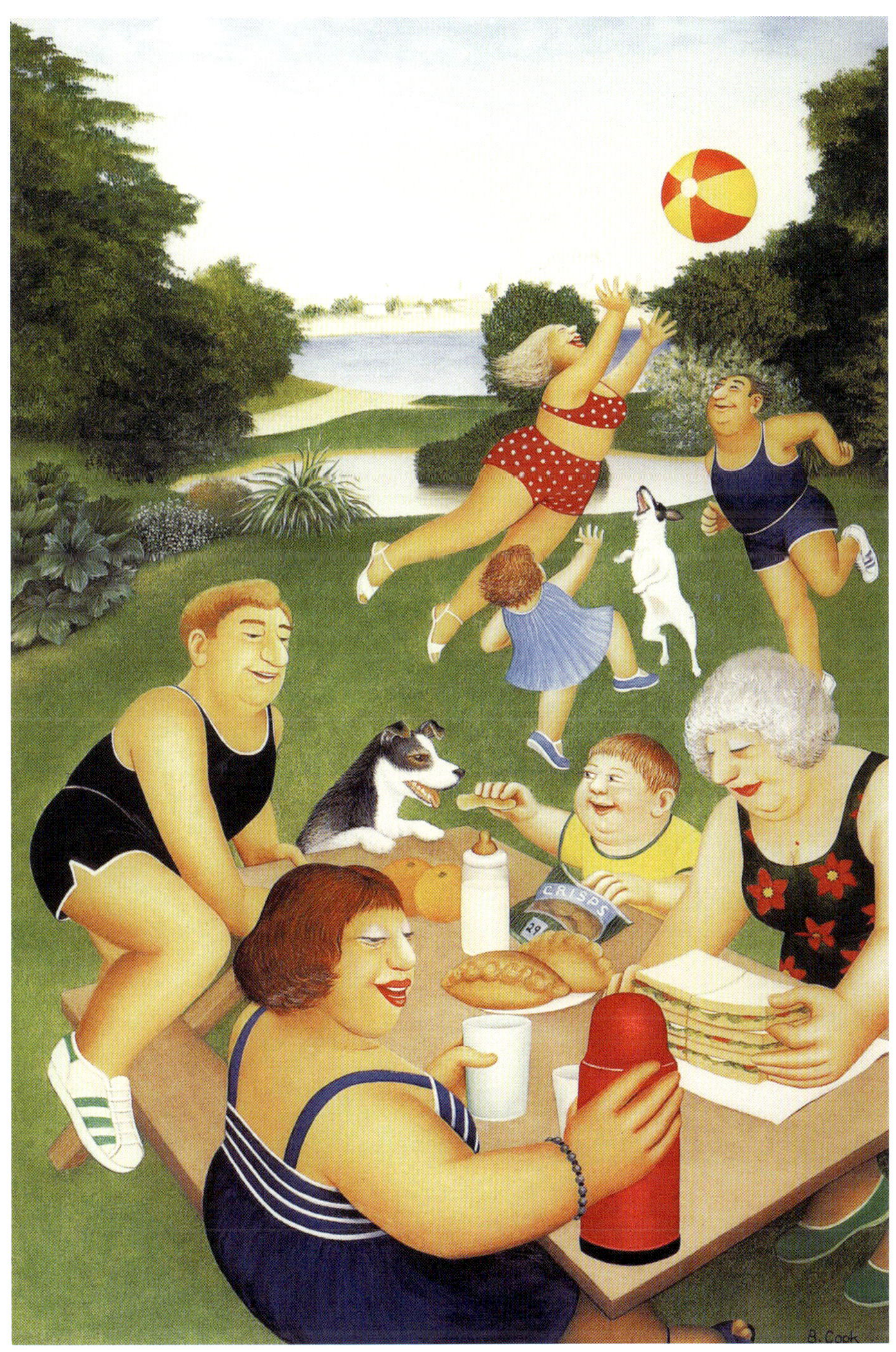

Picnic at Mount Edgcumbe
1991

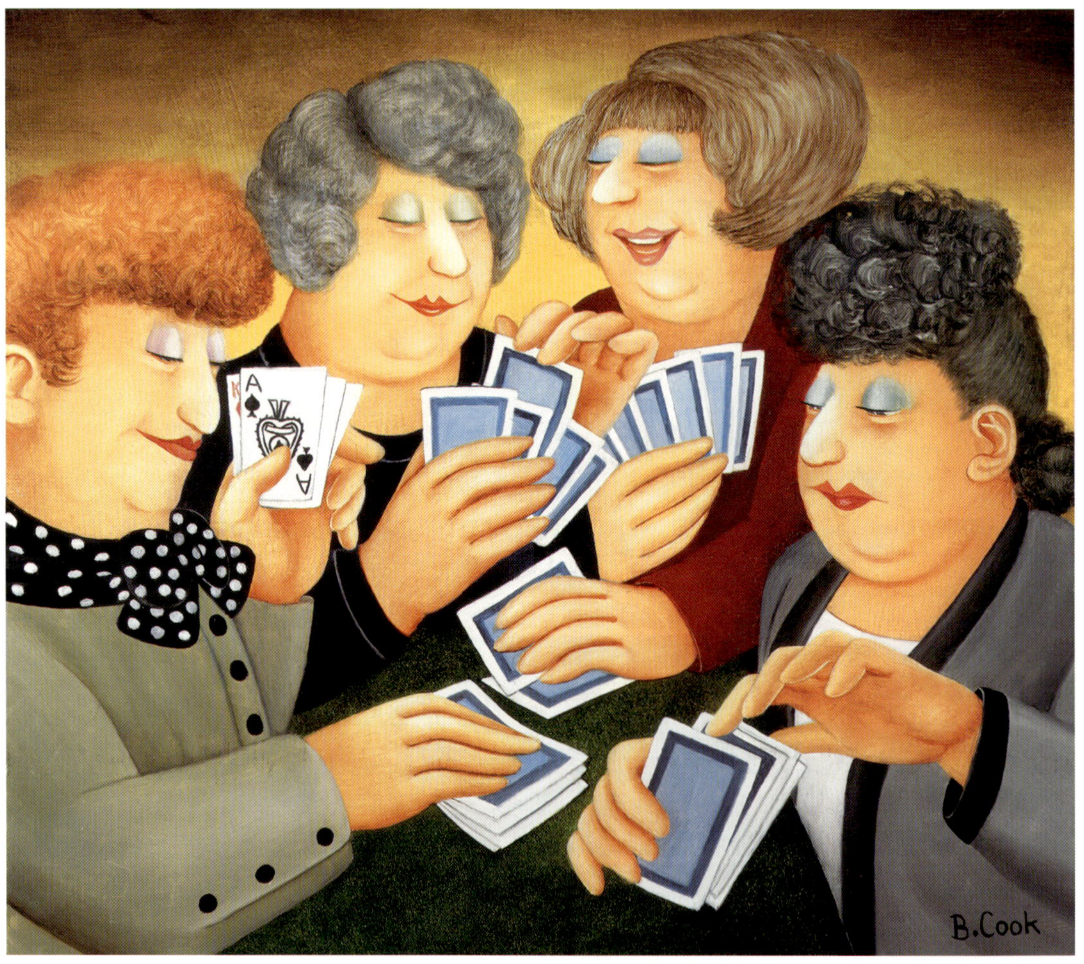

Full House
2004

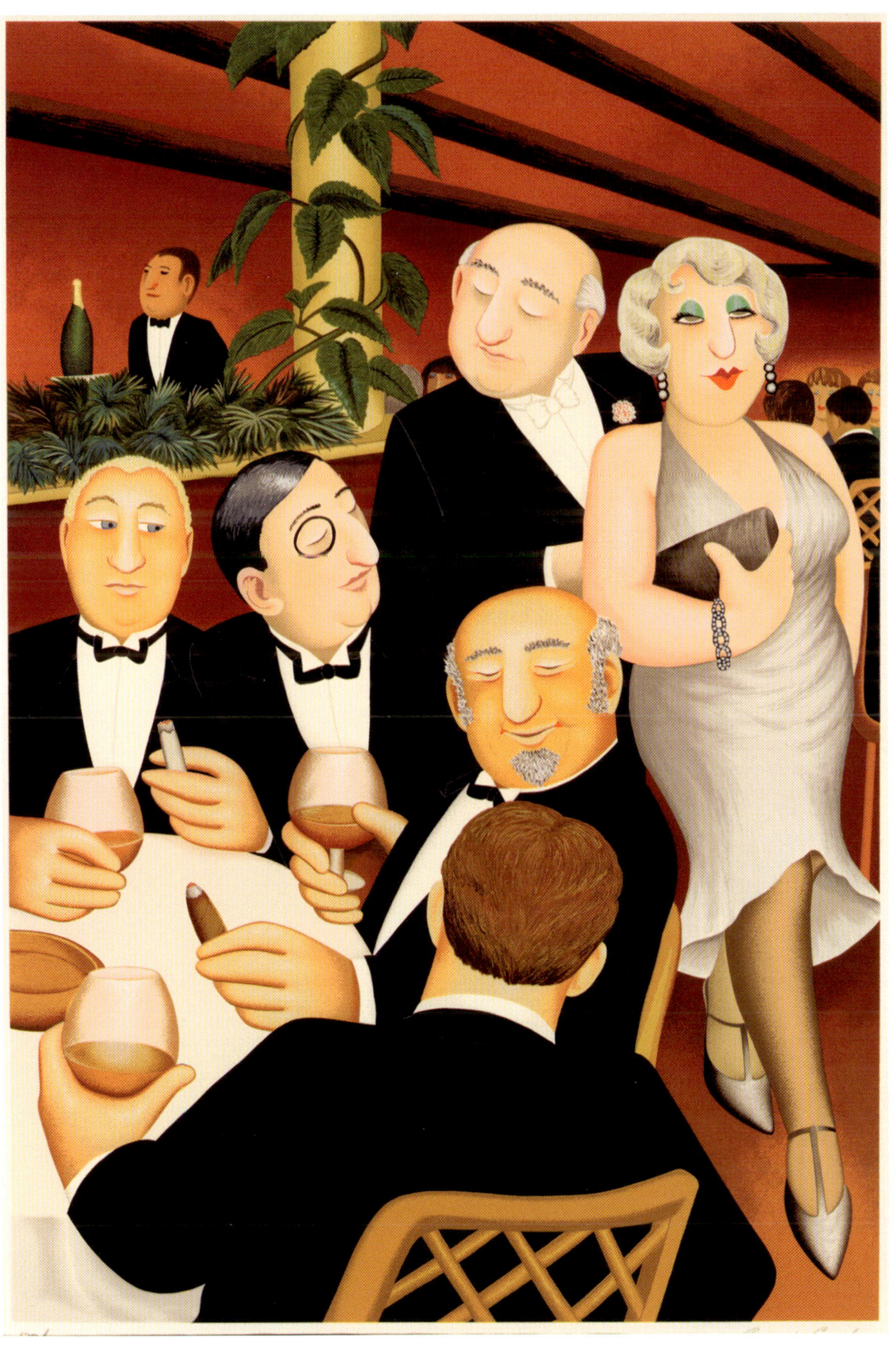

The Baron Entertains
1990

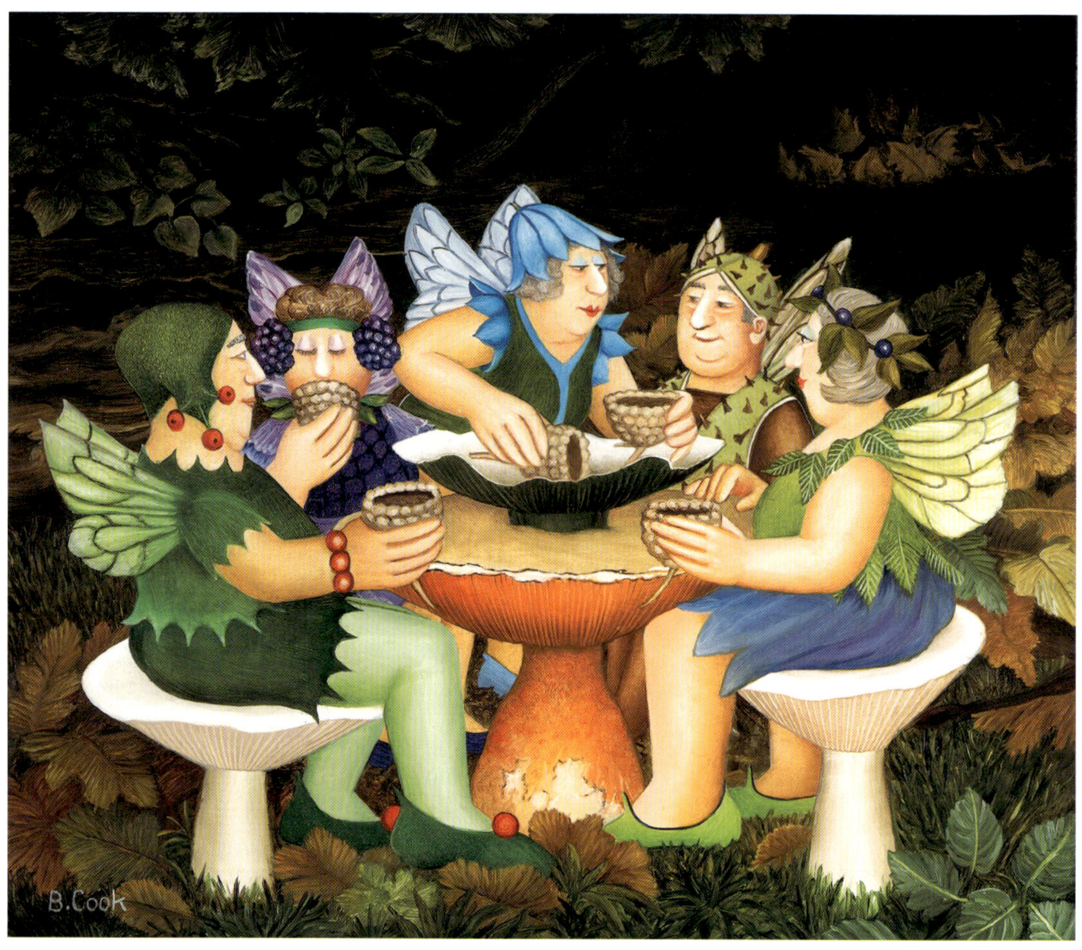

Tasting the Dew Nouveau
2001

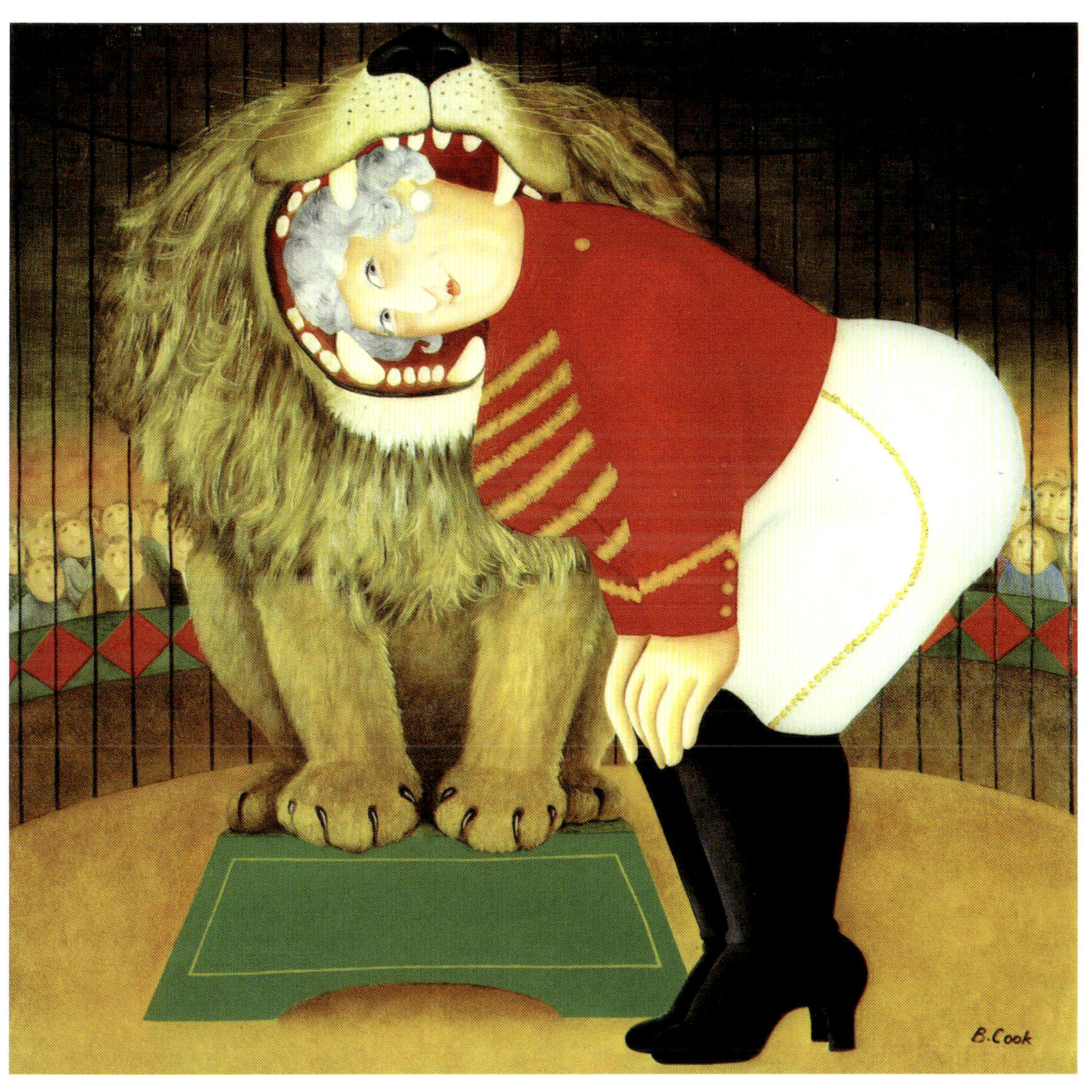

Granny and the Lion
1981

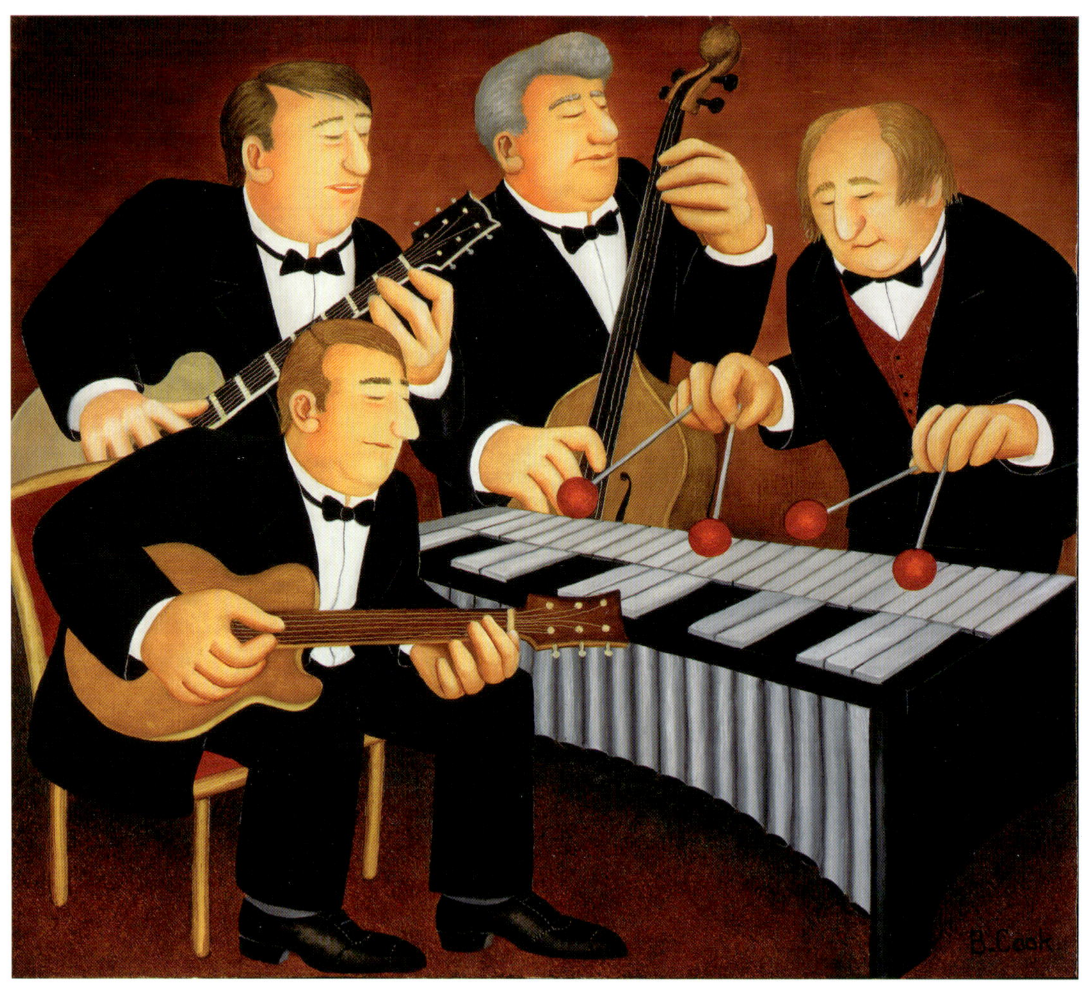

Bernie and the Vibes
2004

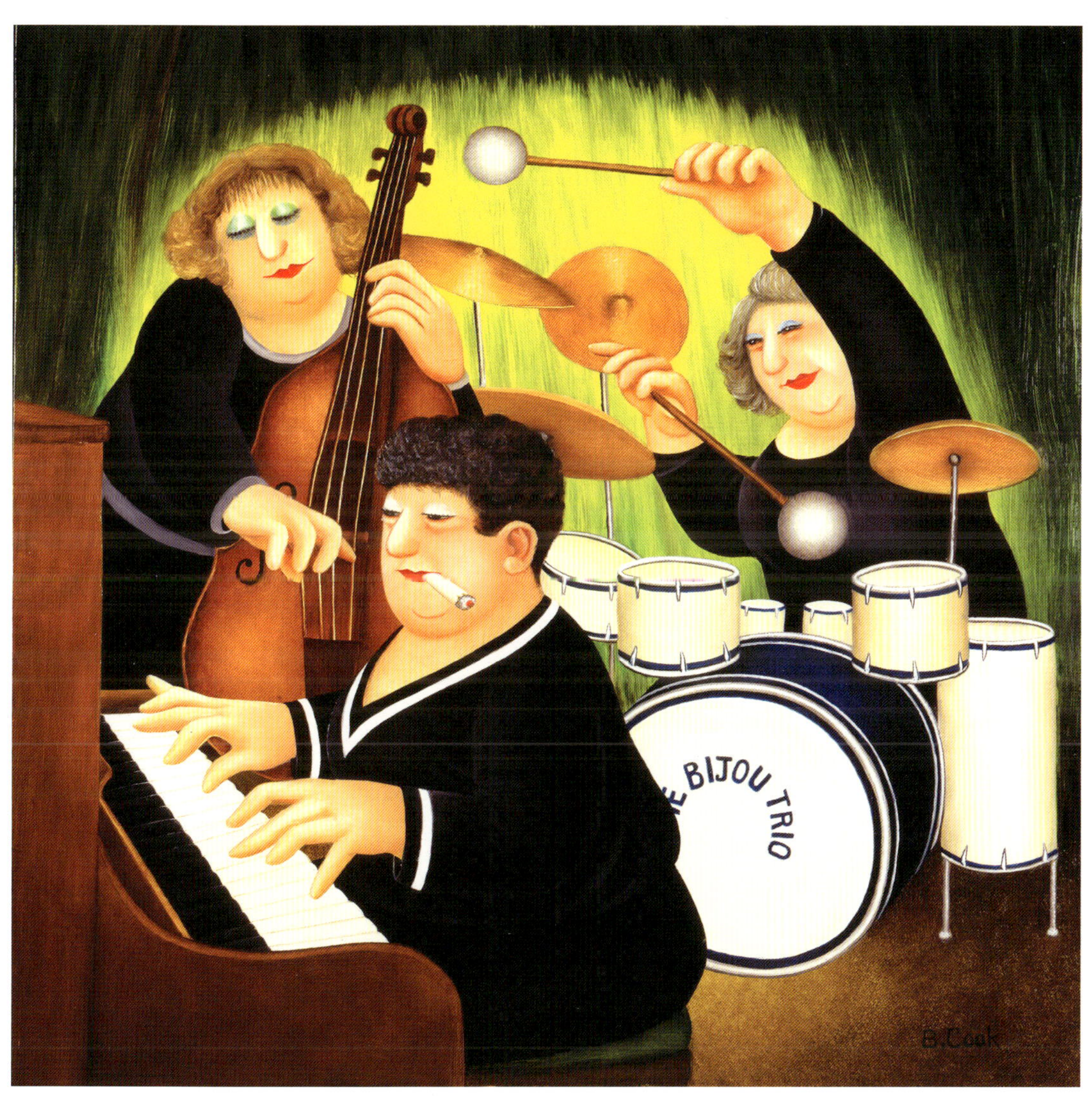

The Bijou Trio
1997

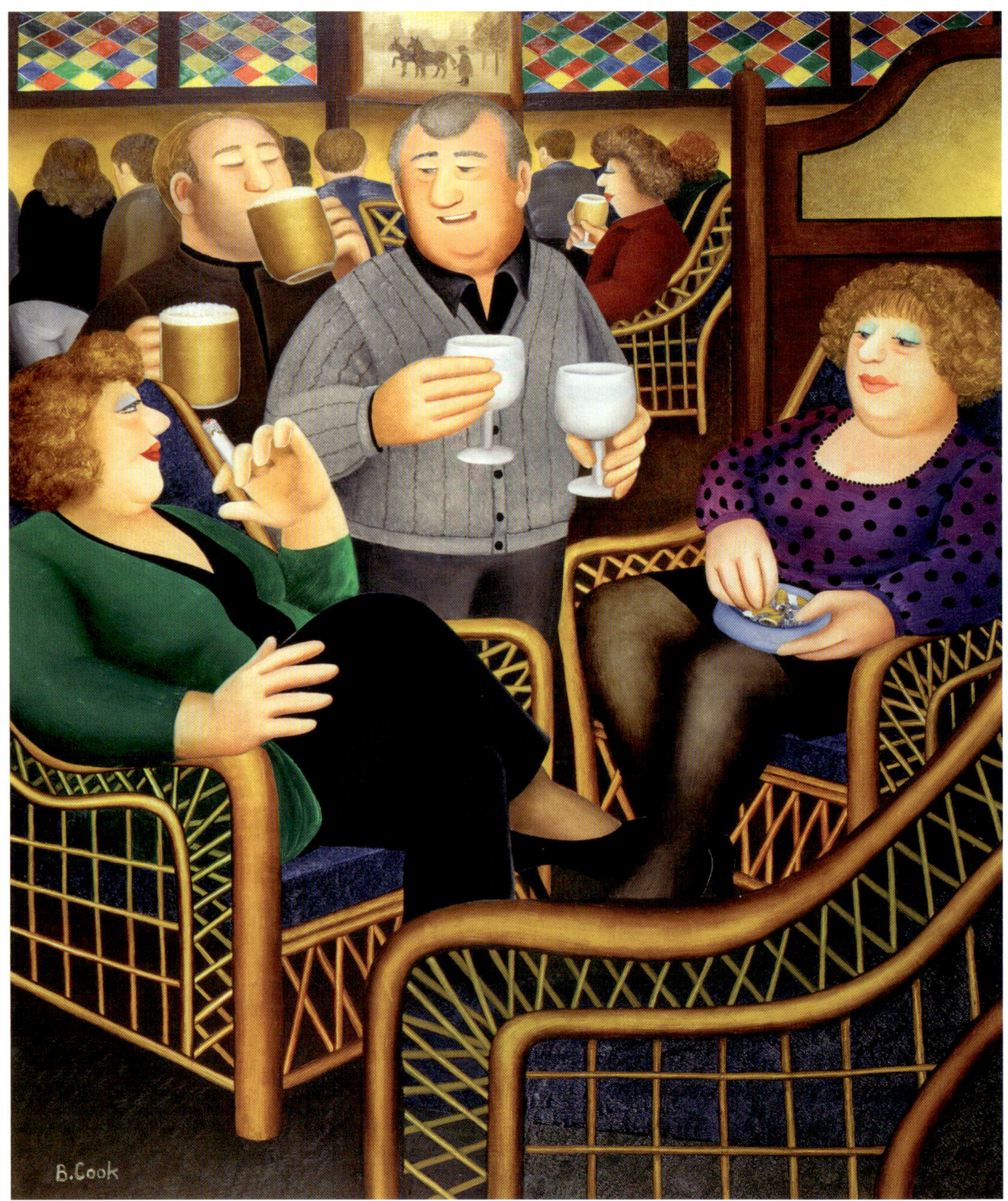

Basket Chairs
1997

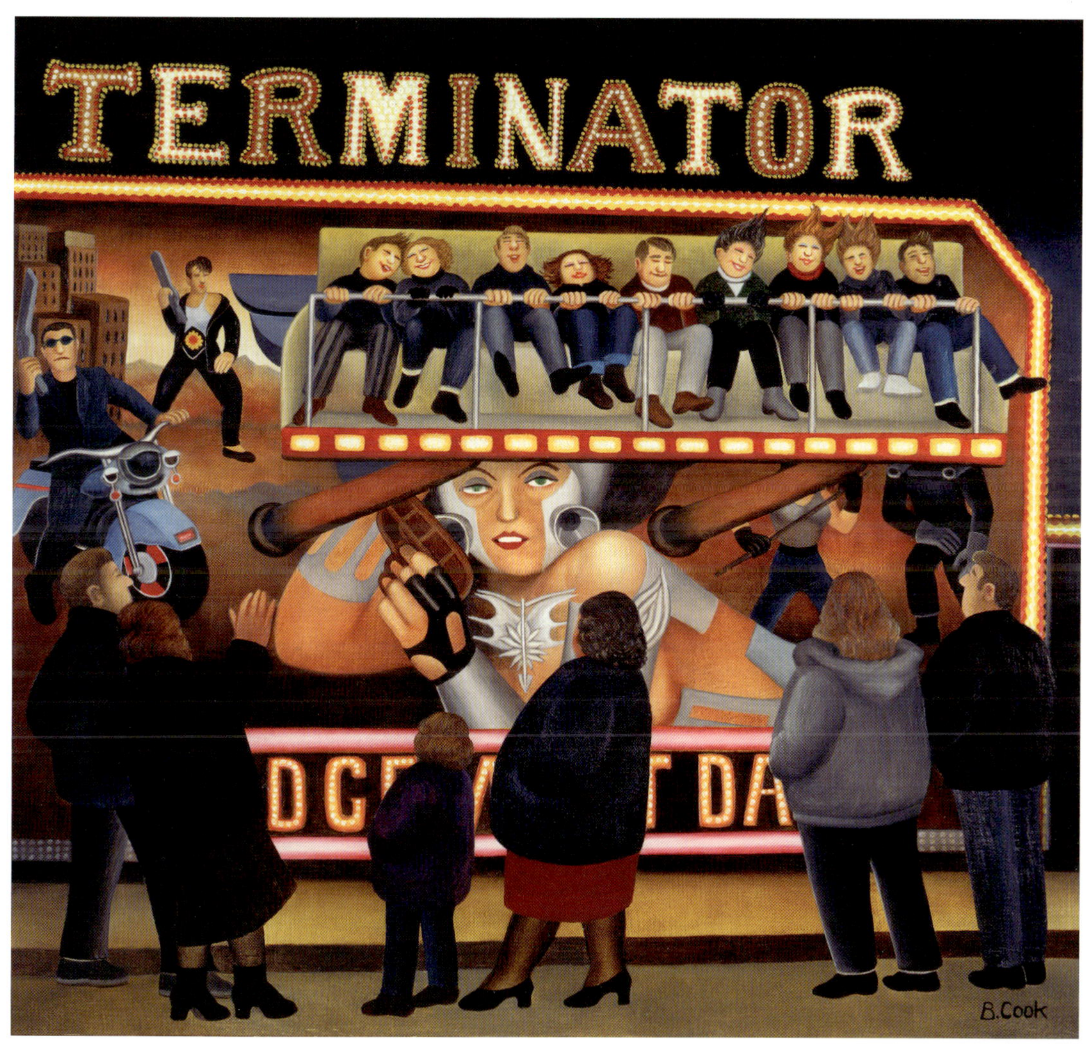

Terminator
1997

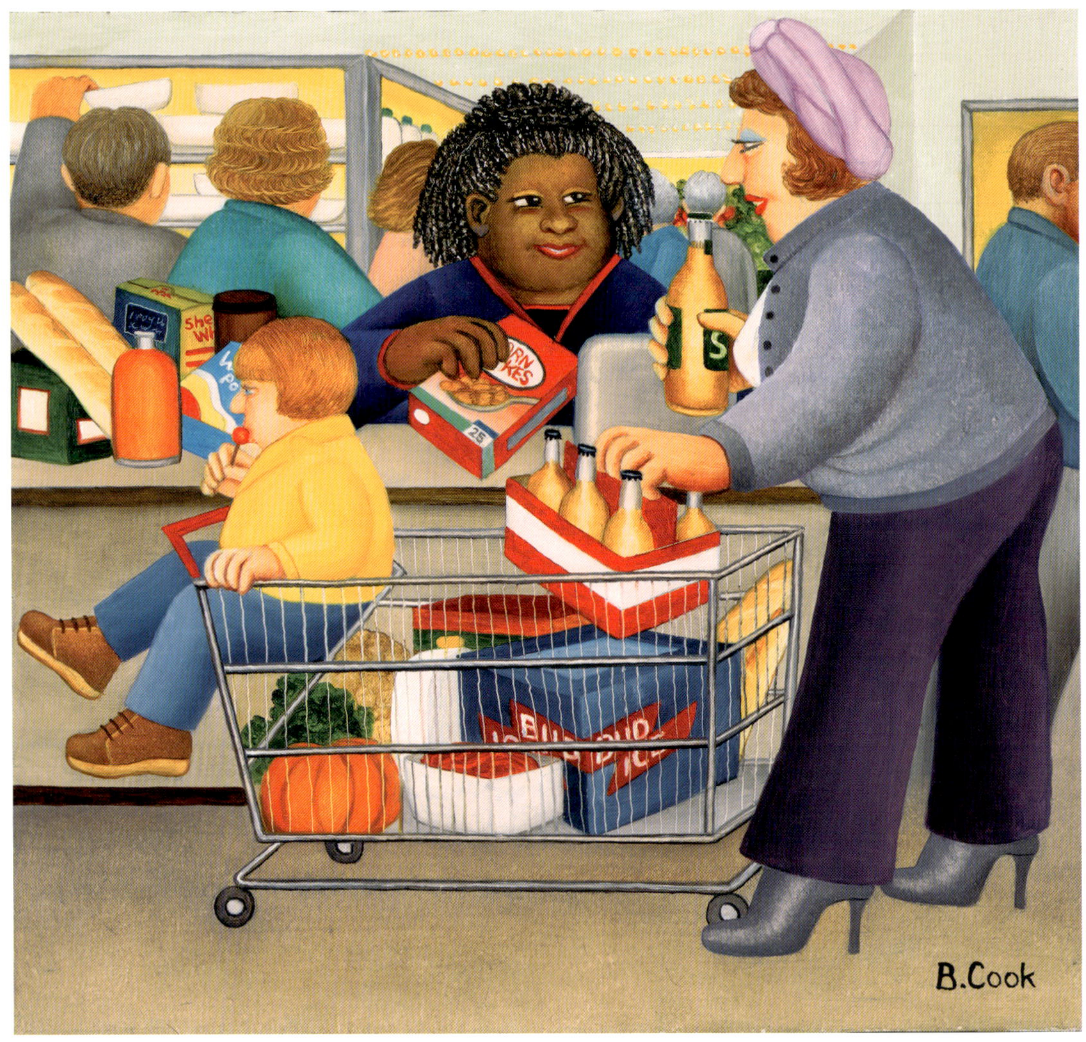

Checking Out
2004

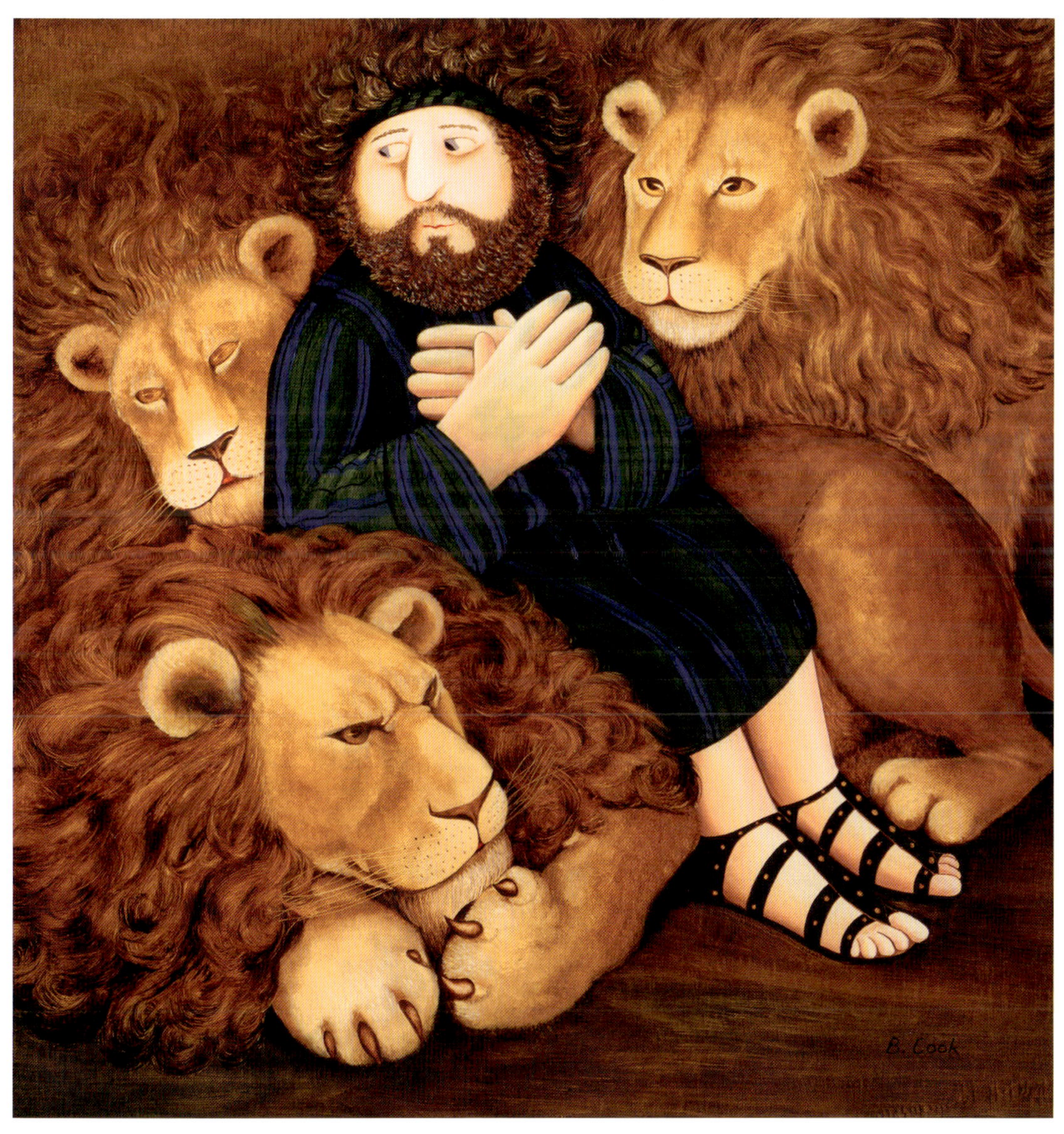

Daniel in the Lion's Den
1980

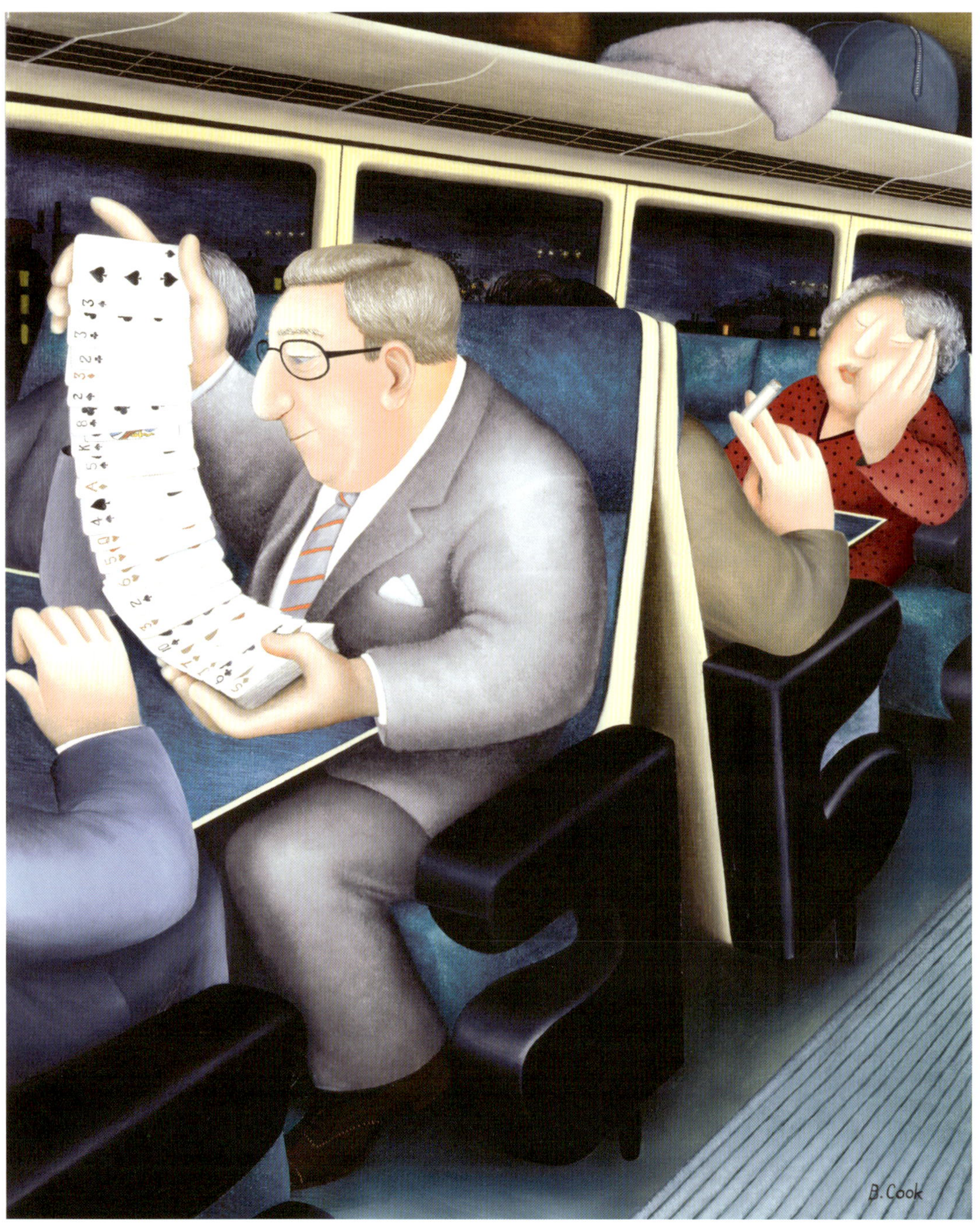

The Fan Shuffle
1988

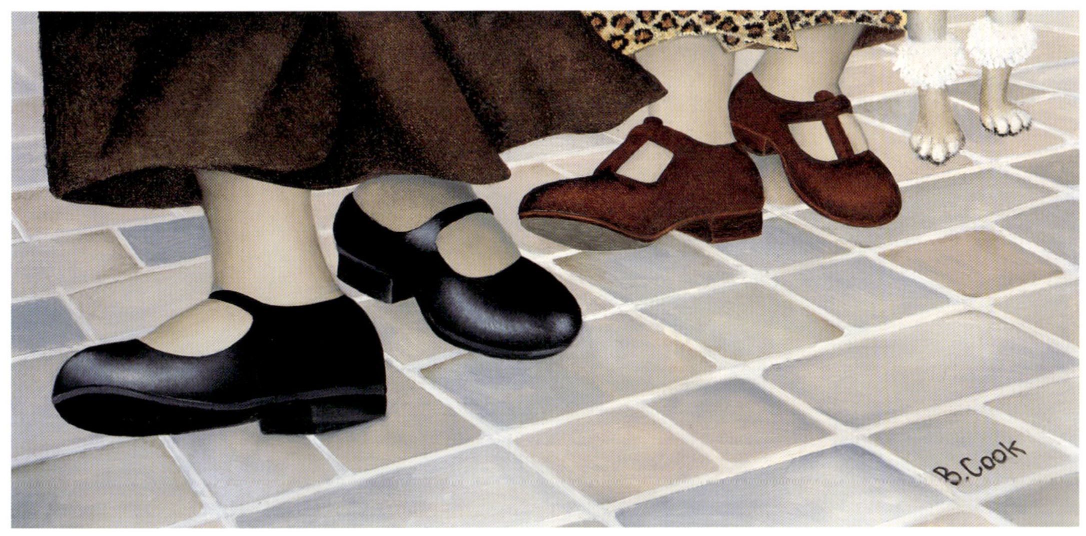

Gertrude's Shoes
2006

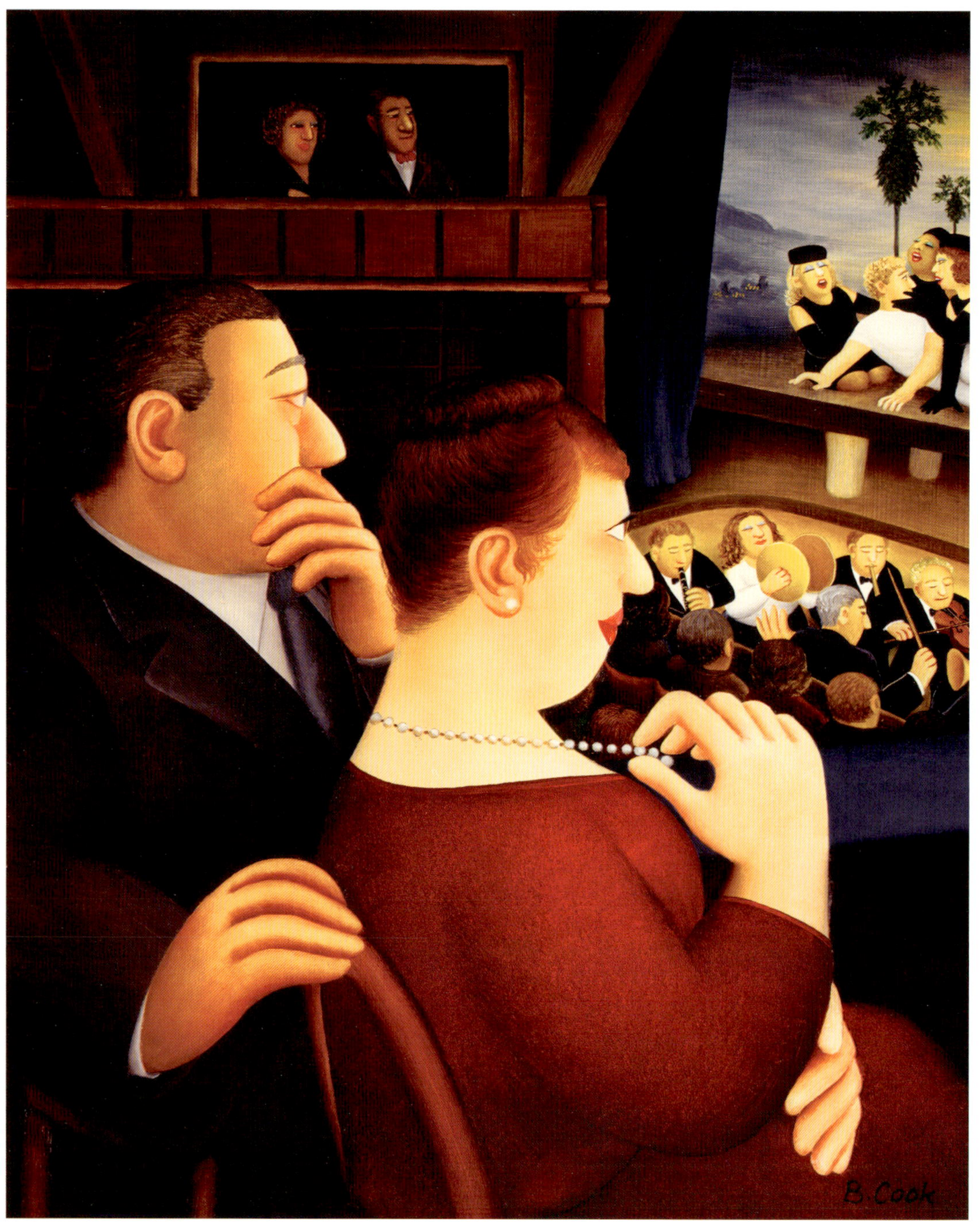

A Magical Evening at Glydebourne
1991

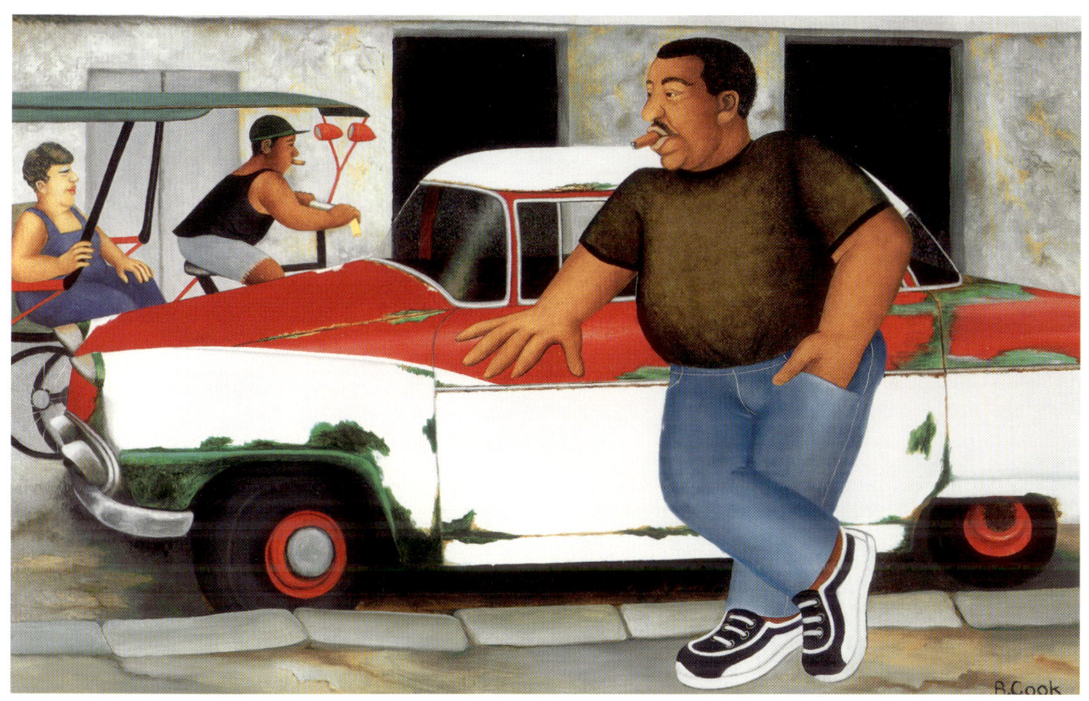

Havana
2000

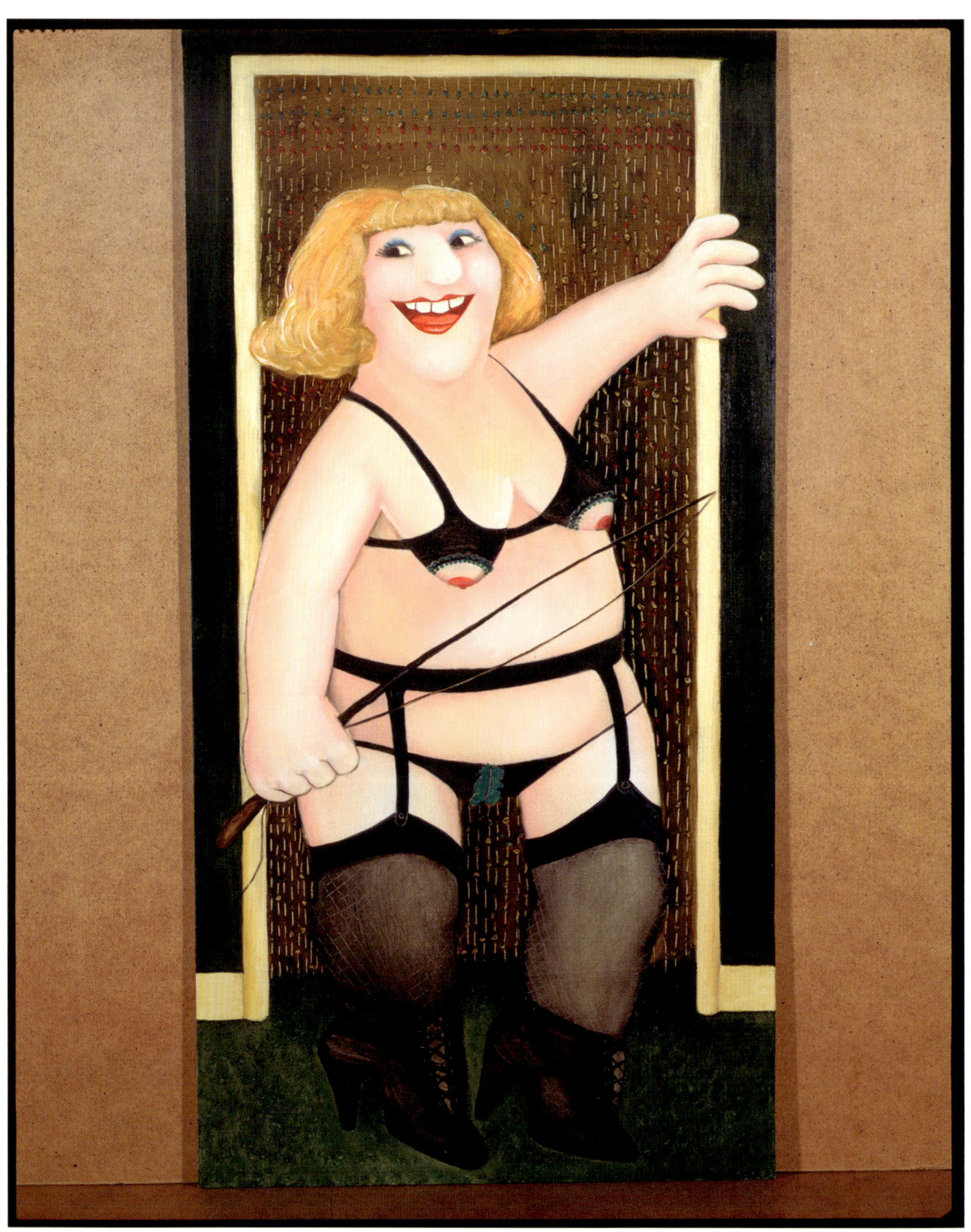

Anyone for a Whipping?
1972

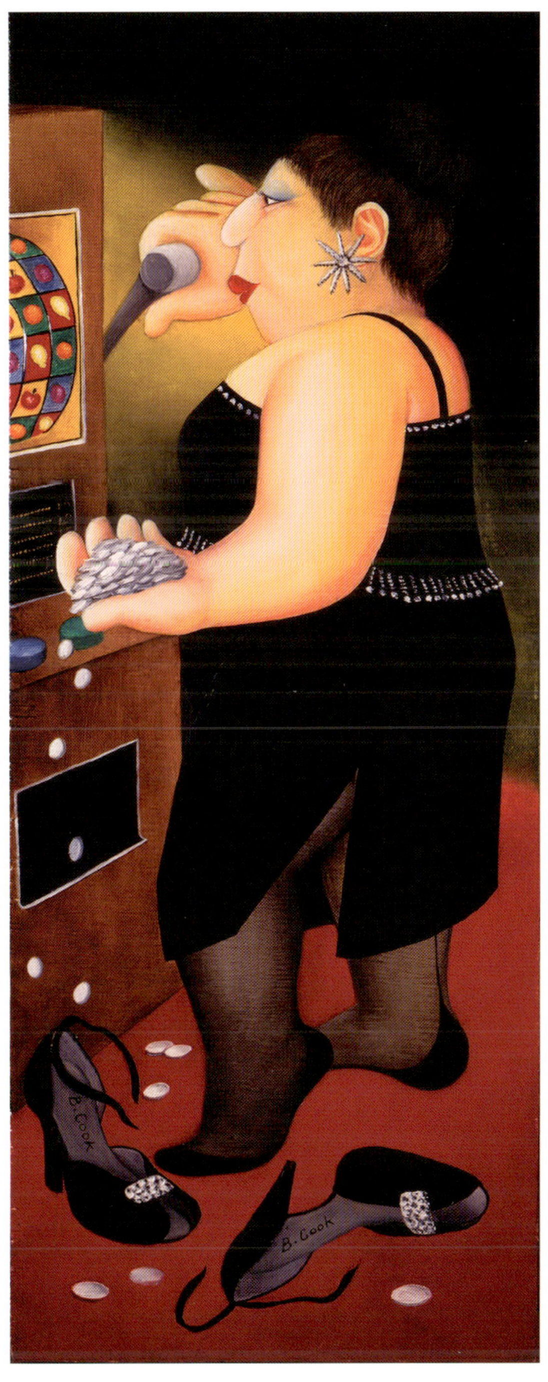

Jackpot
1980

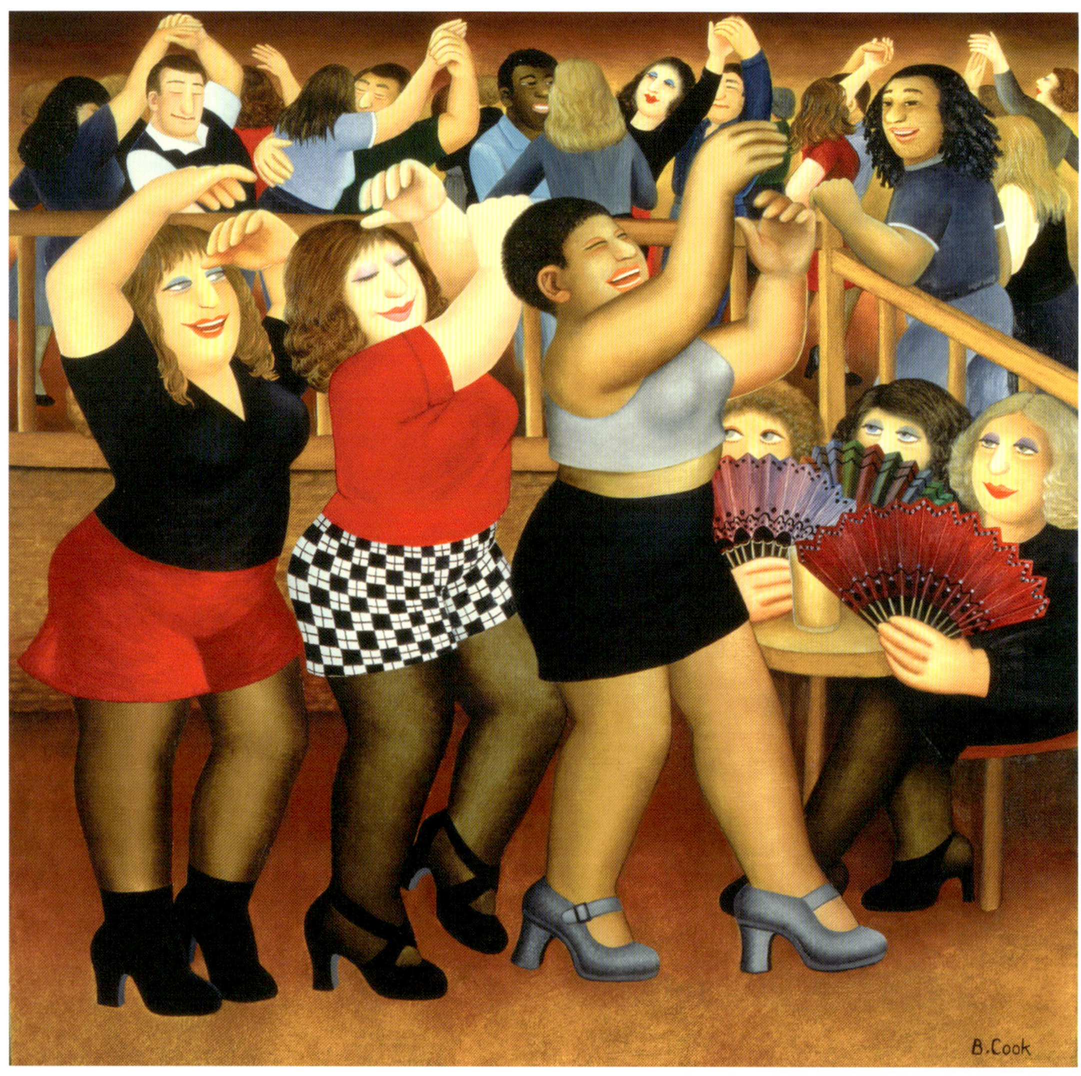

Doing the Lambada
1997

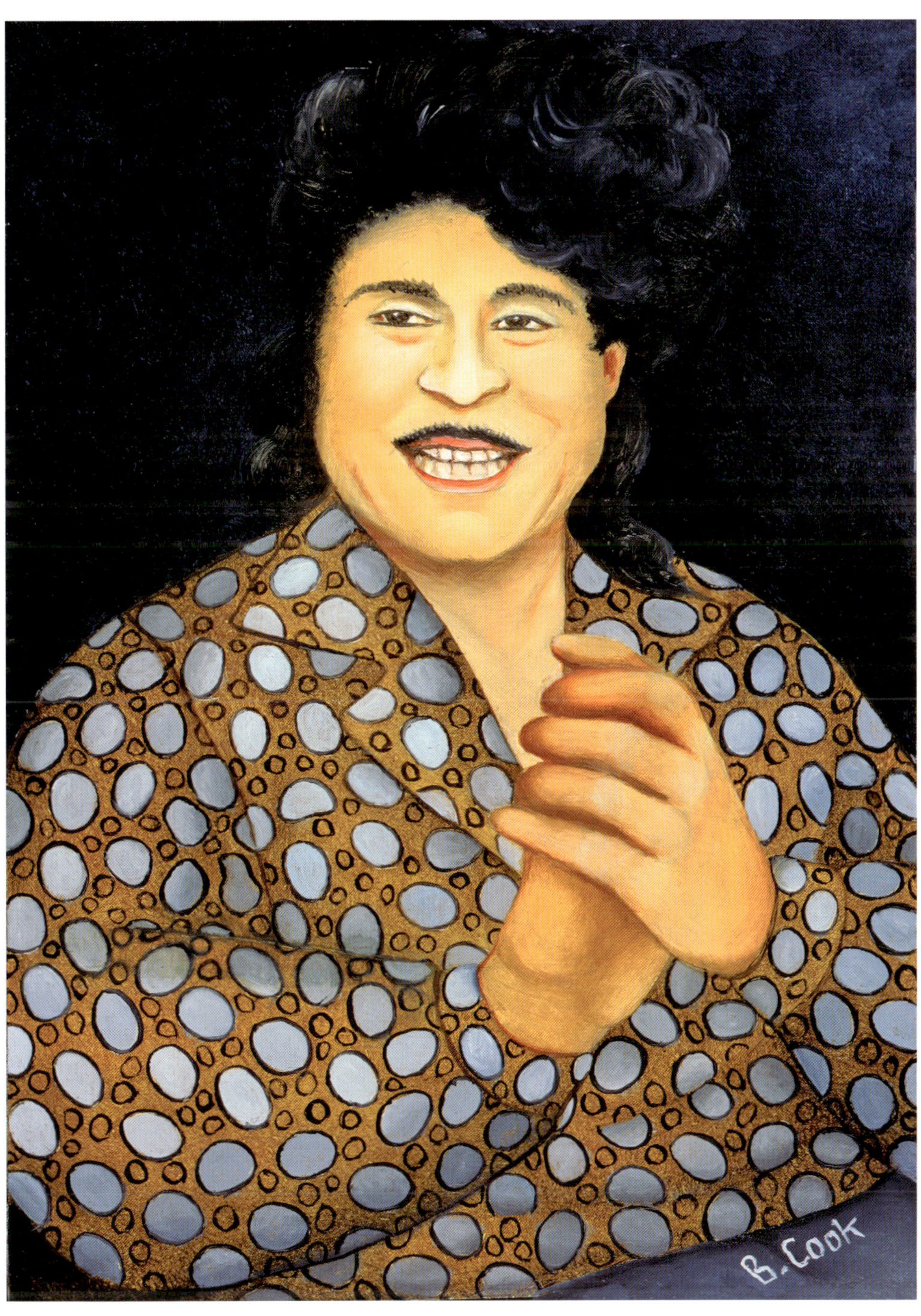

Little Richard
2003

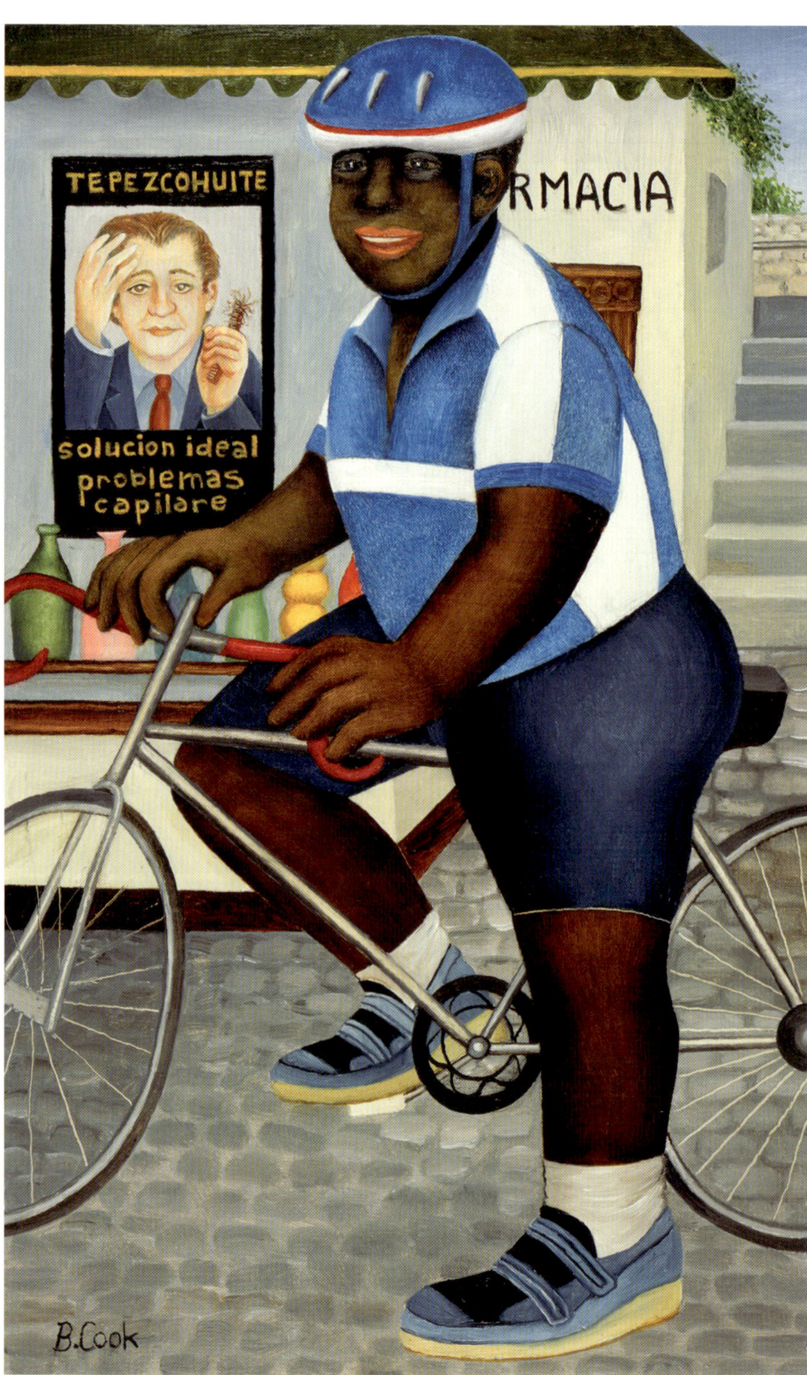

Los Colista
2004

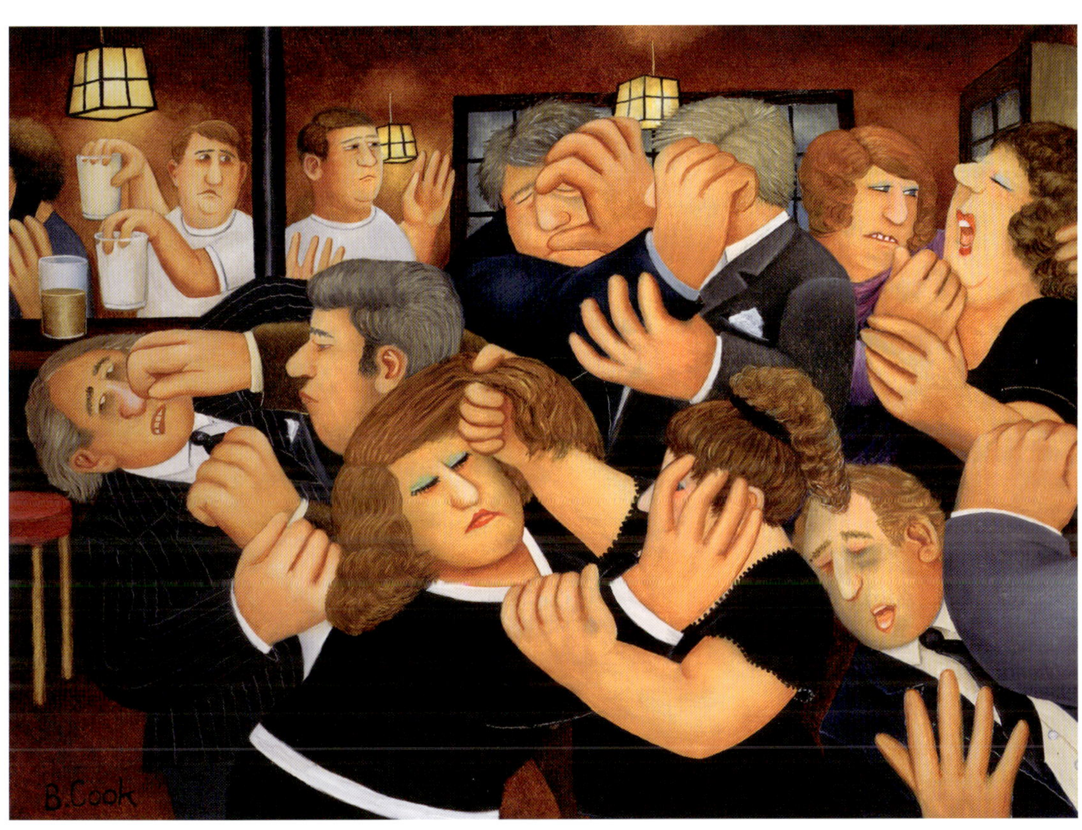

The Wake
2005

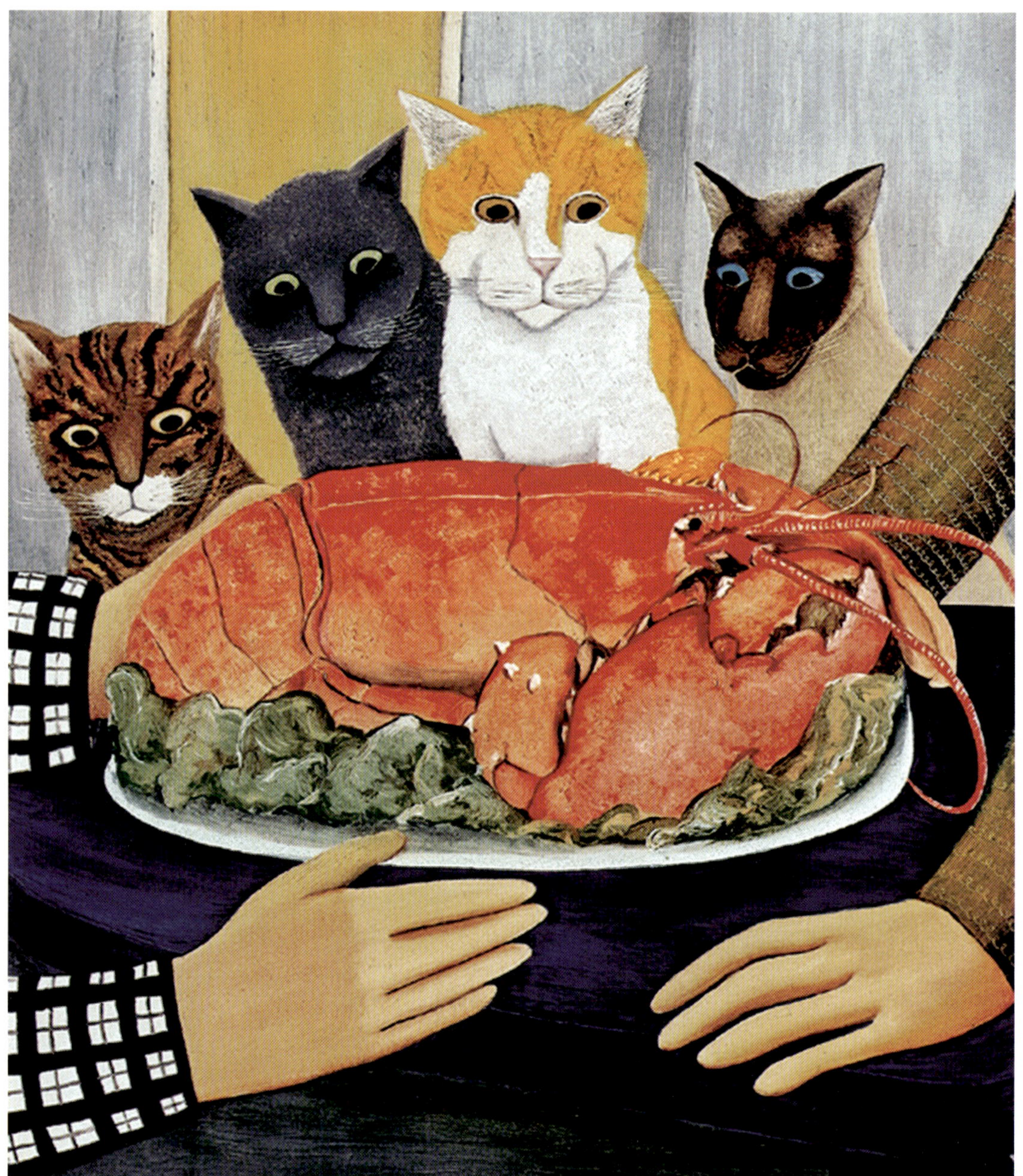

Four Hungry Cats
circa 1977

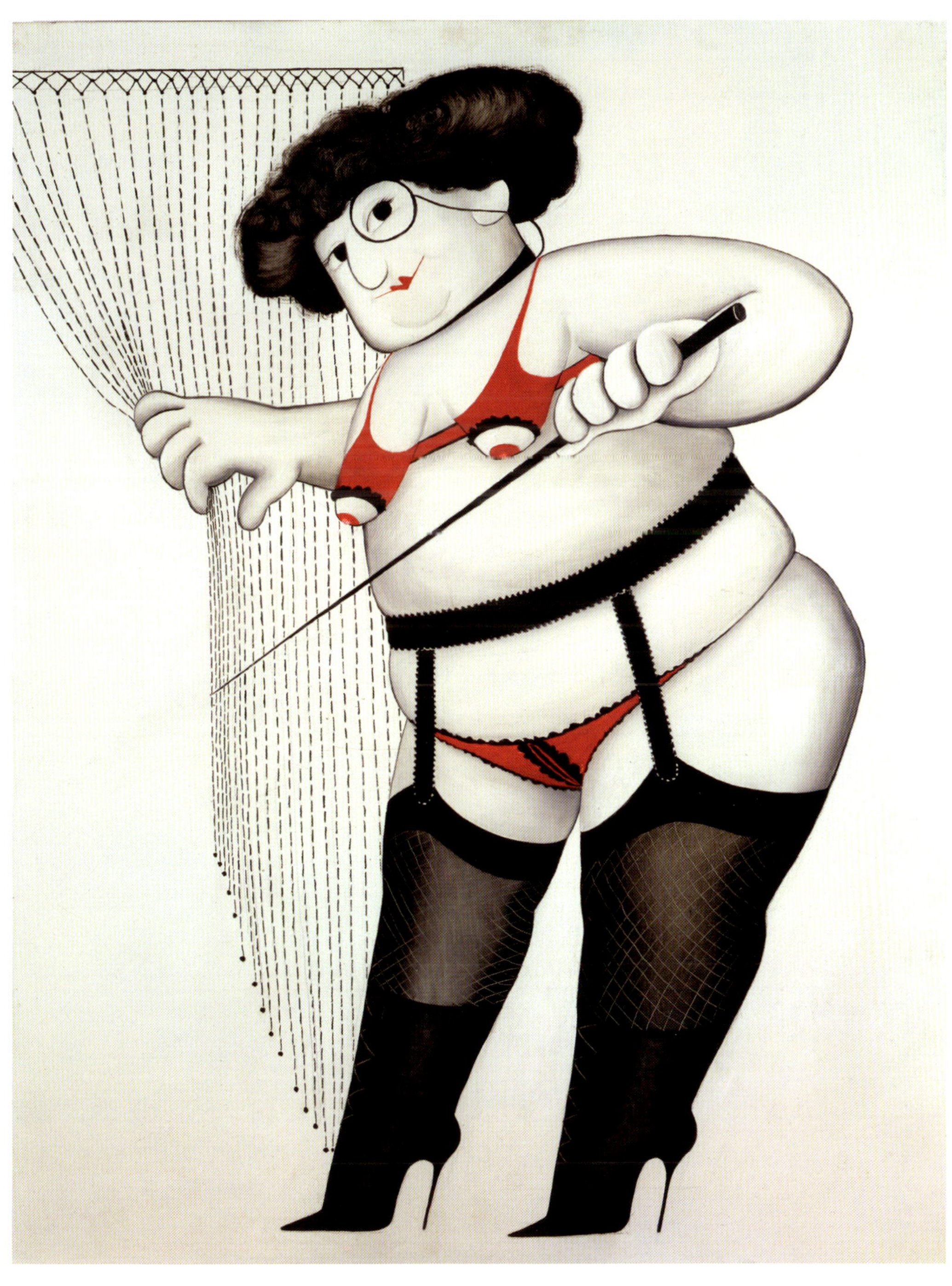

Next!
1975

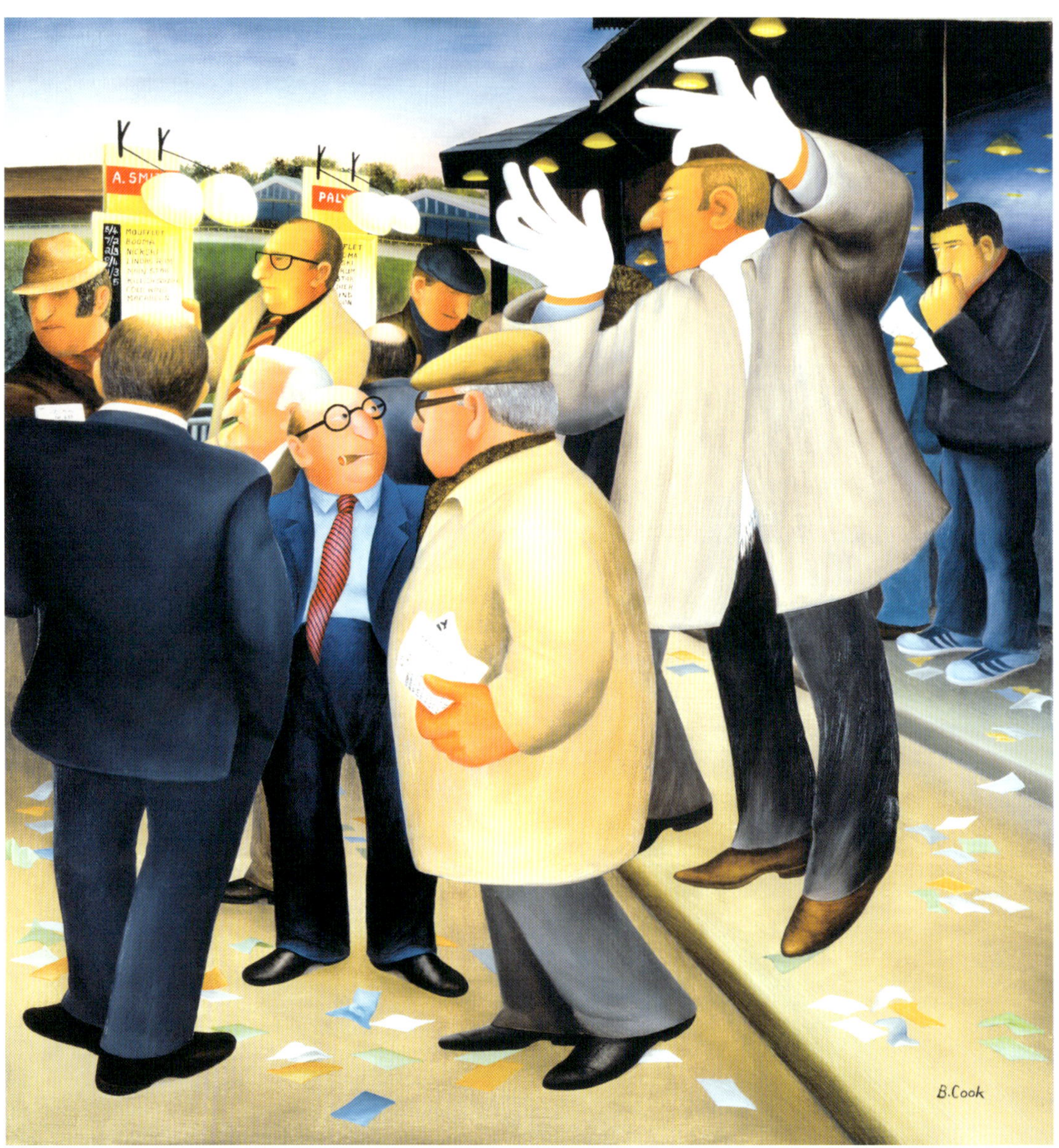

Tic-Tac Man
1987

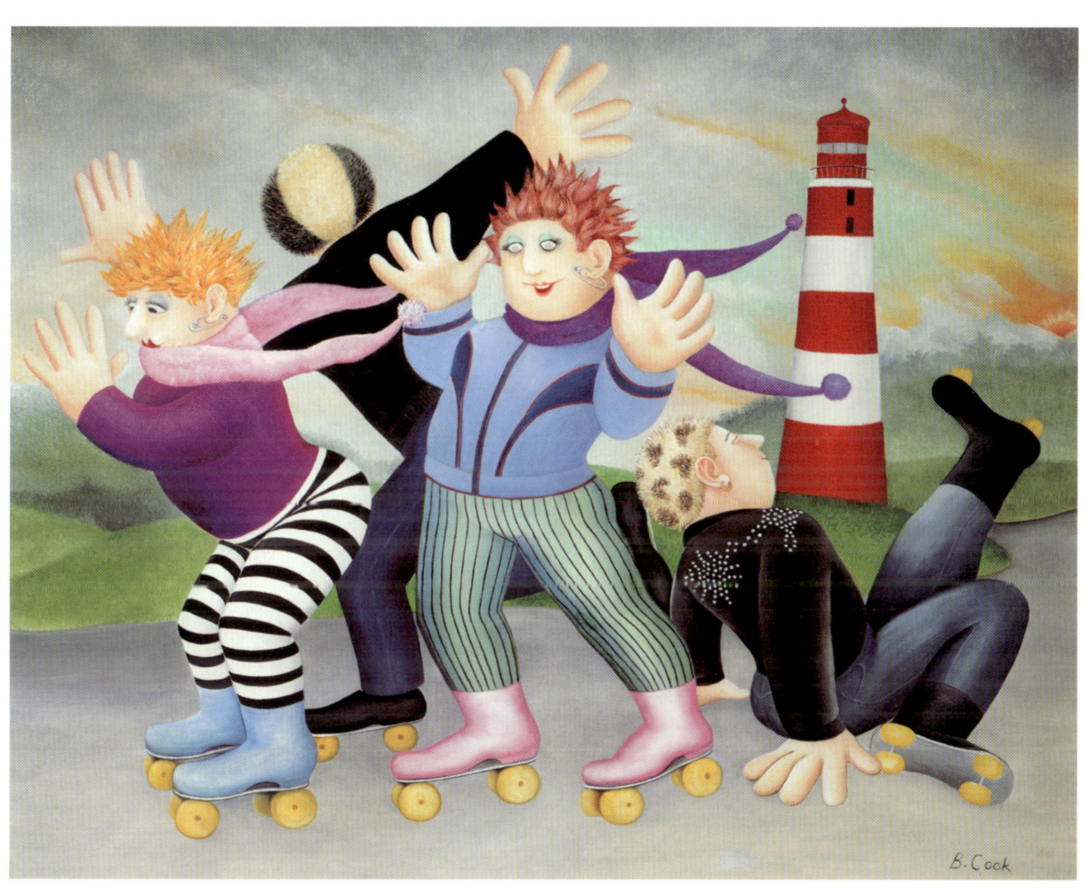

Punks on Plymouth Hoe
1996

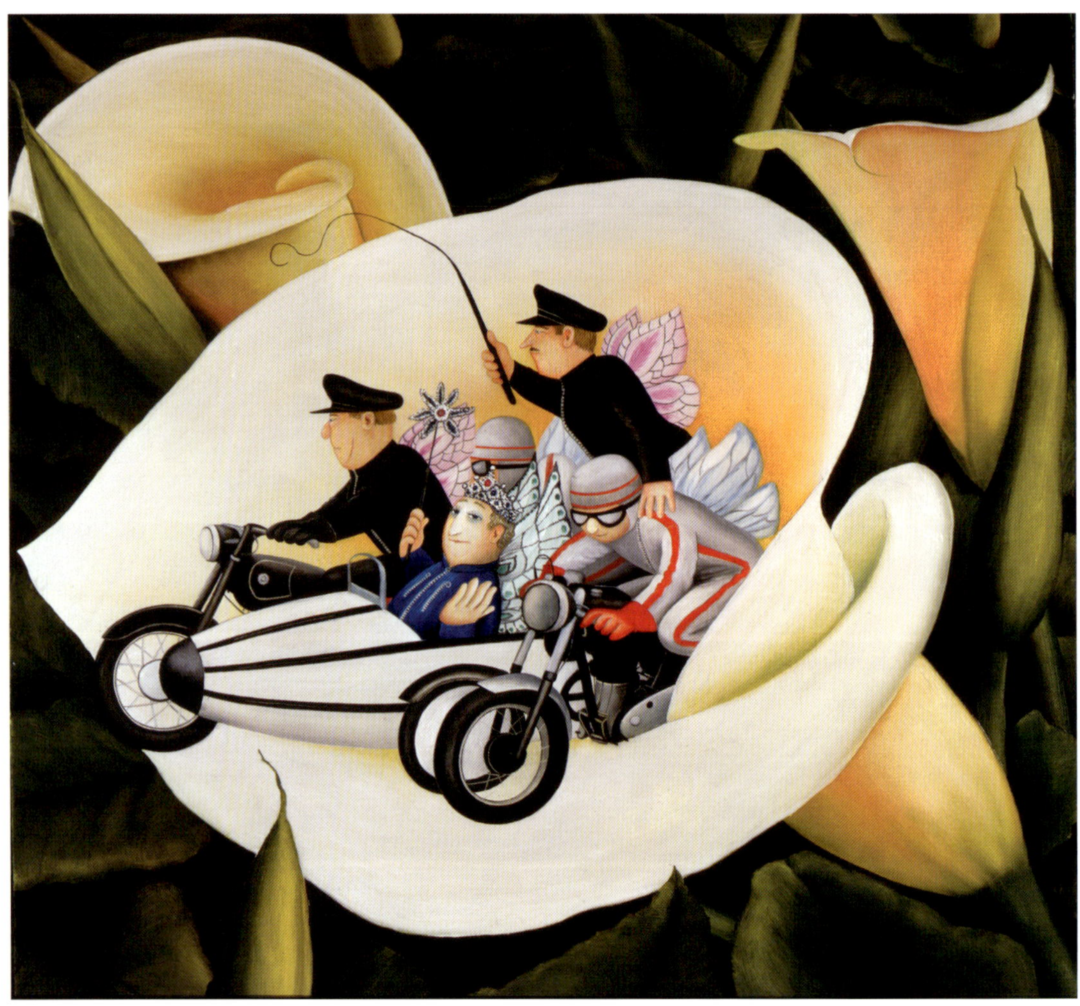

Queen of the Fairies
1980

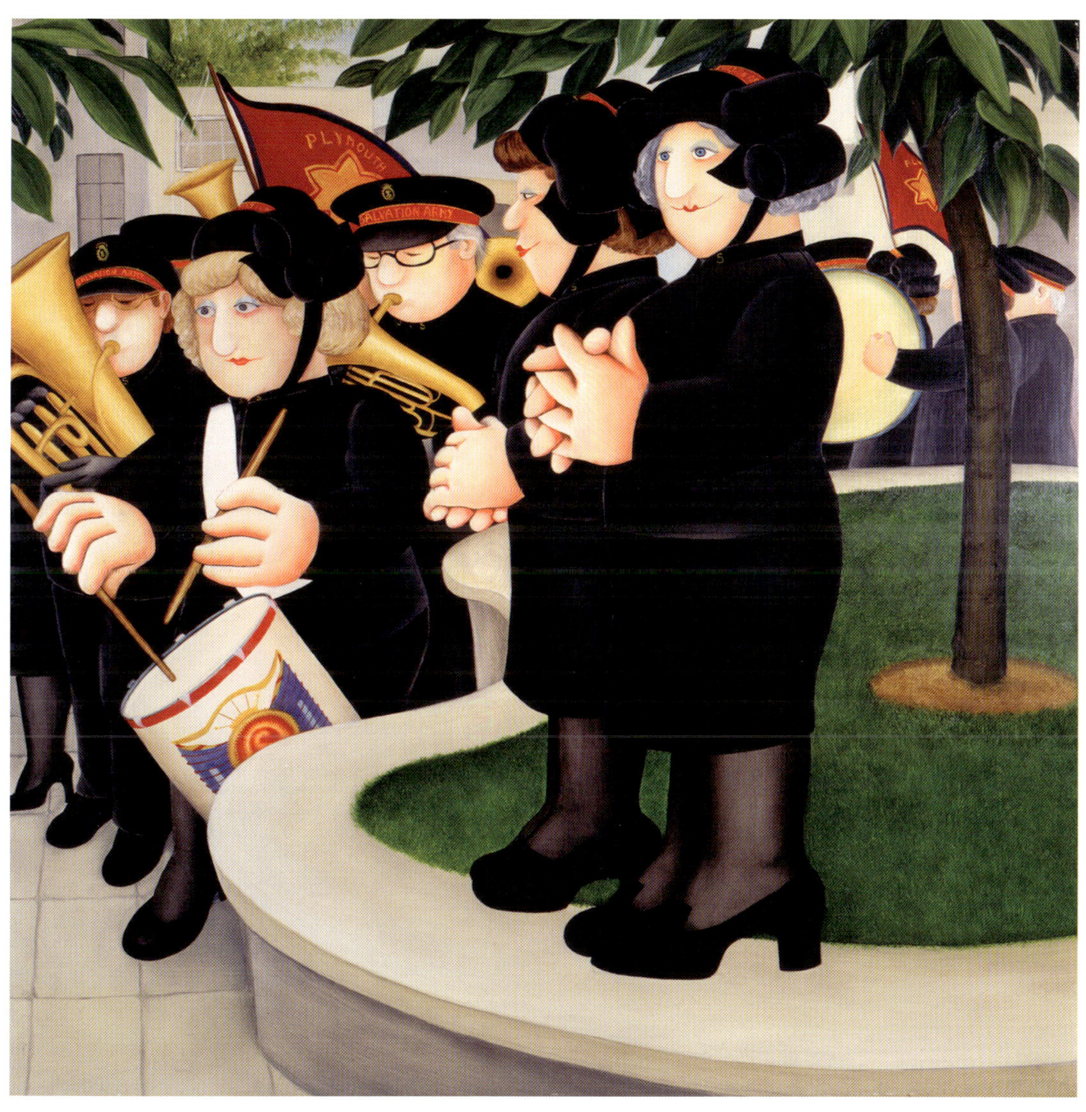

Salvation Army Band
circa 1980

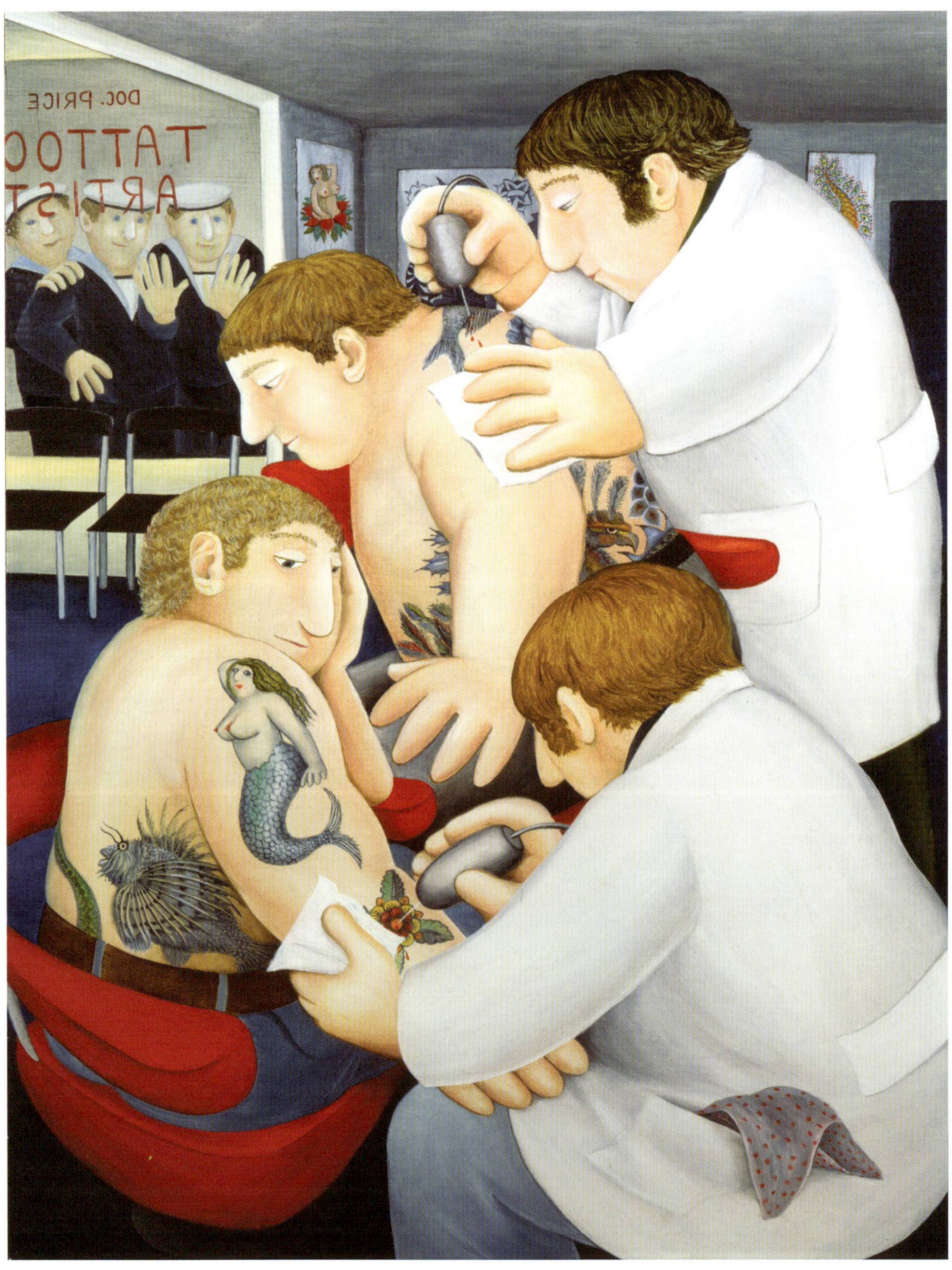

Tattoo Artist
1979

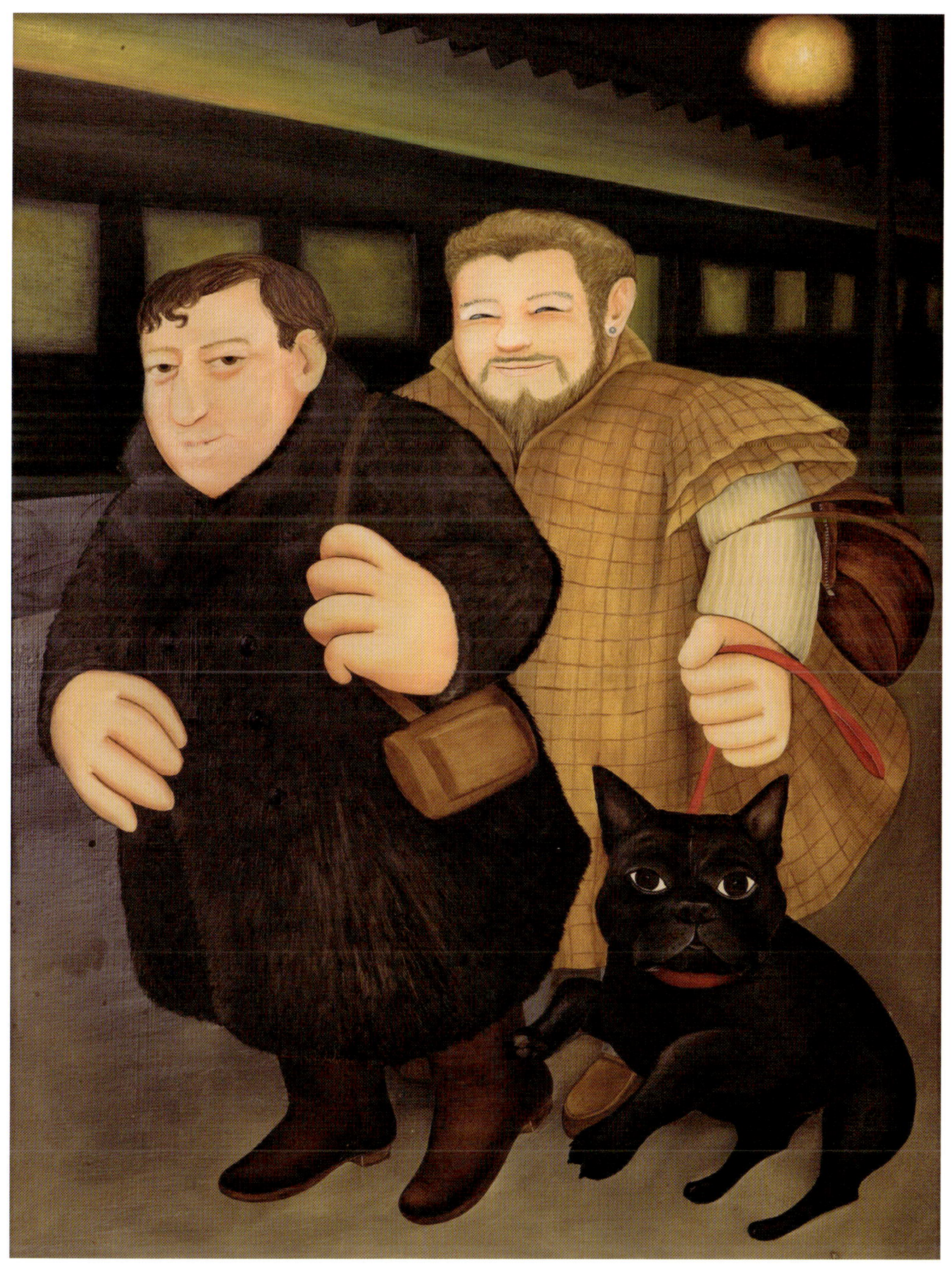

Ted and Heinrich
1979

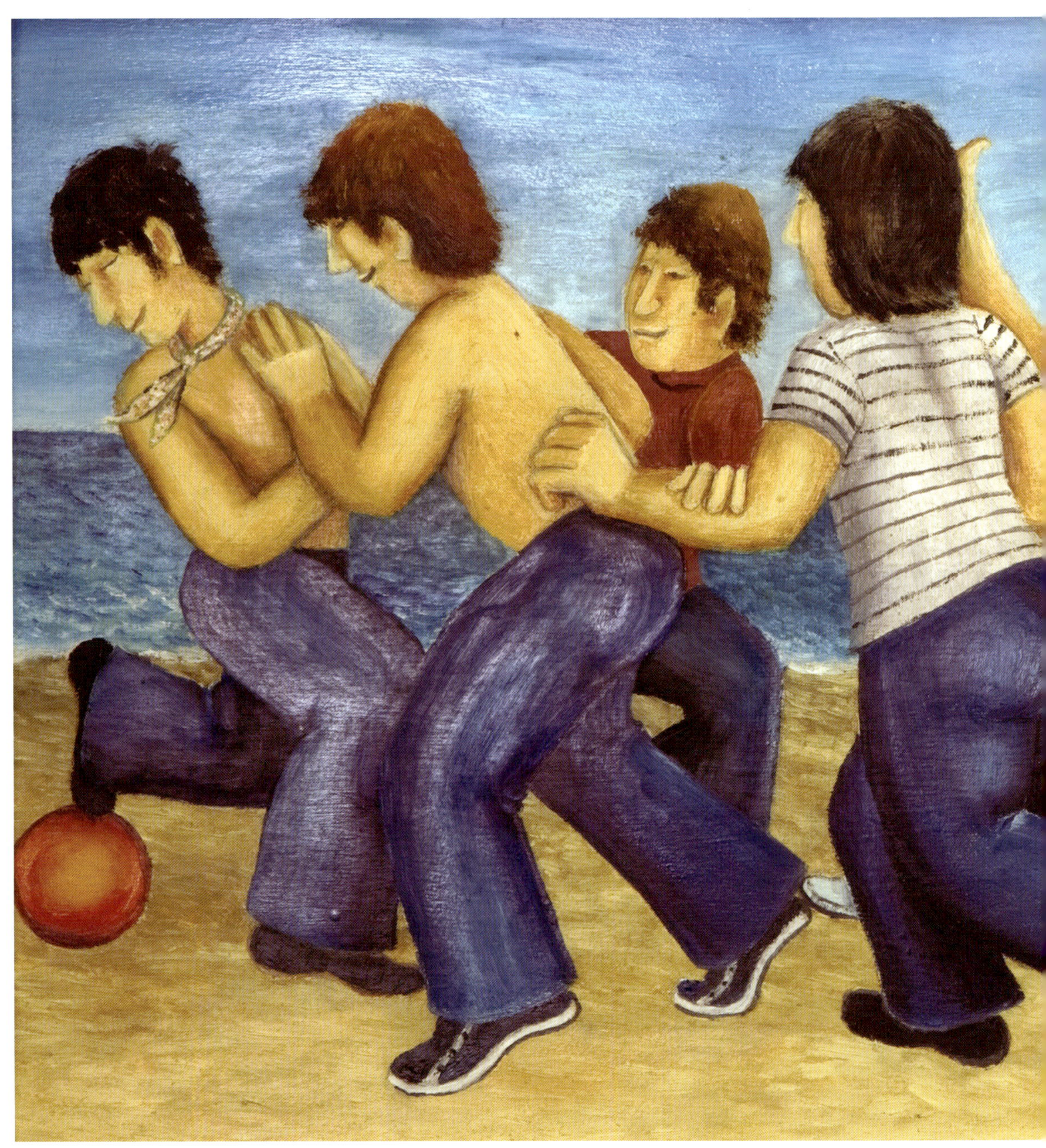

Footballers on the Beach
1966

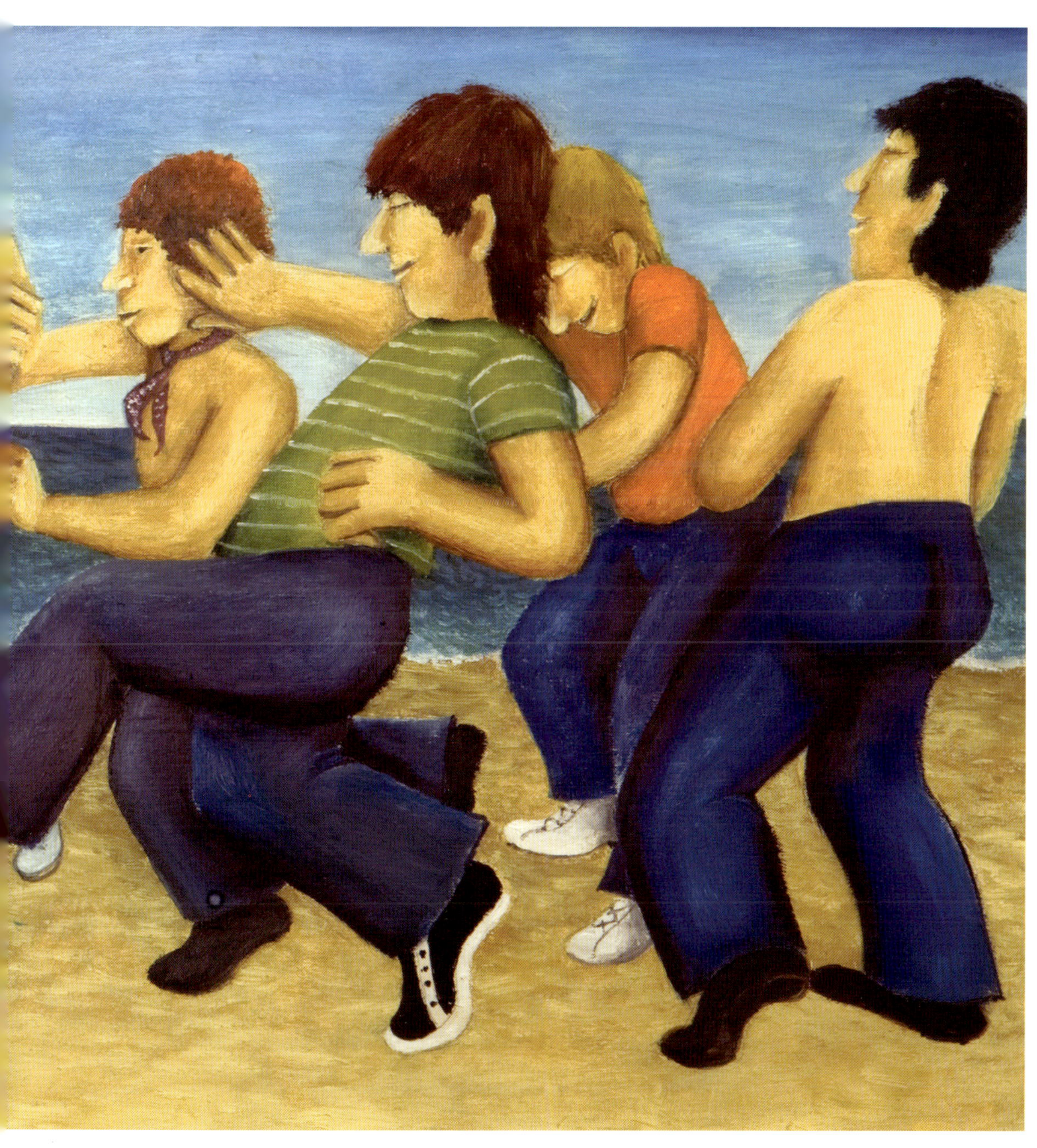

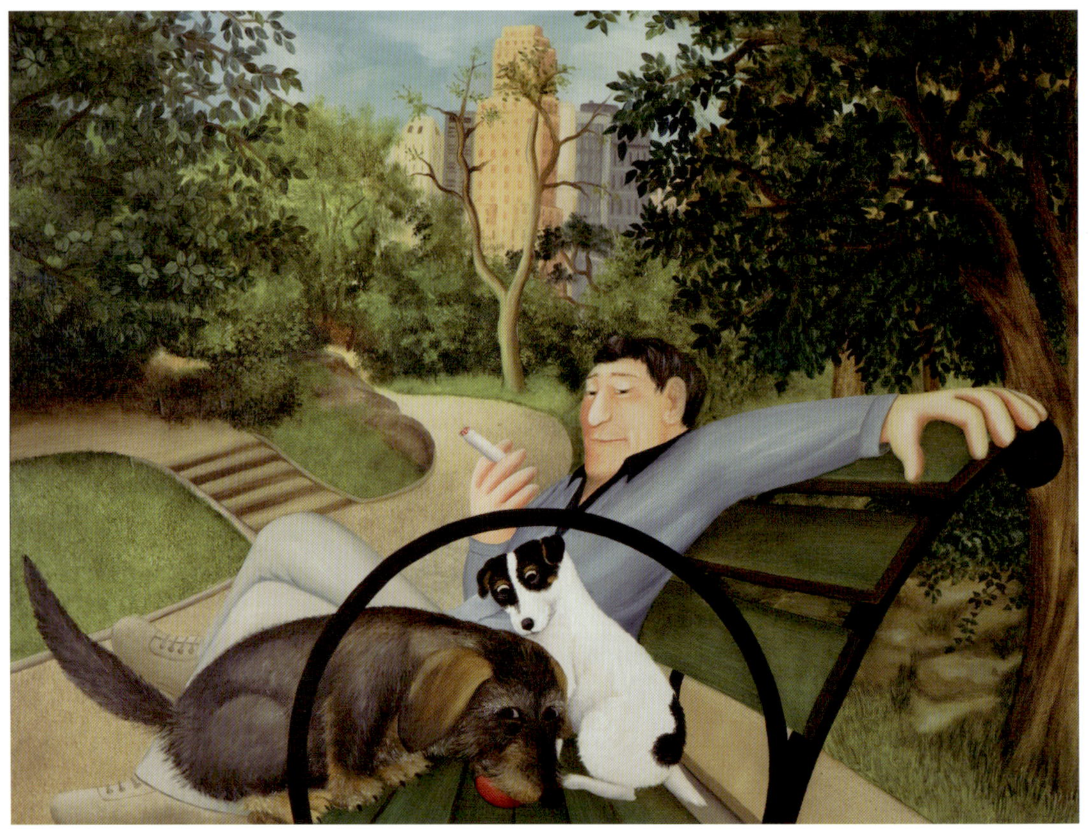

Central Park
1983

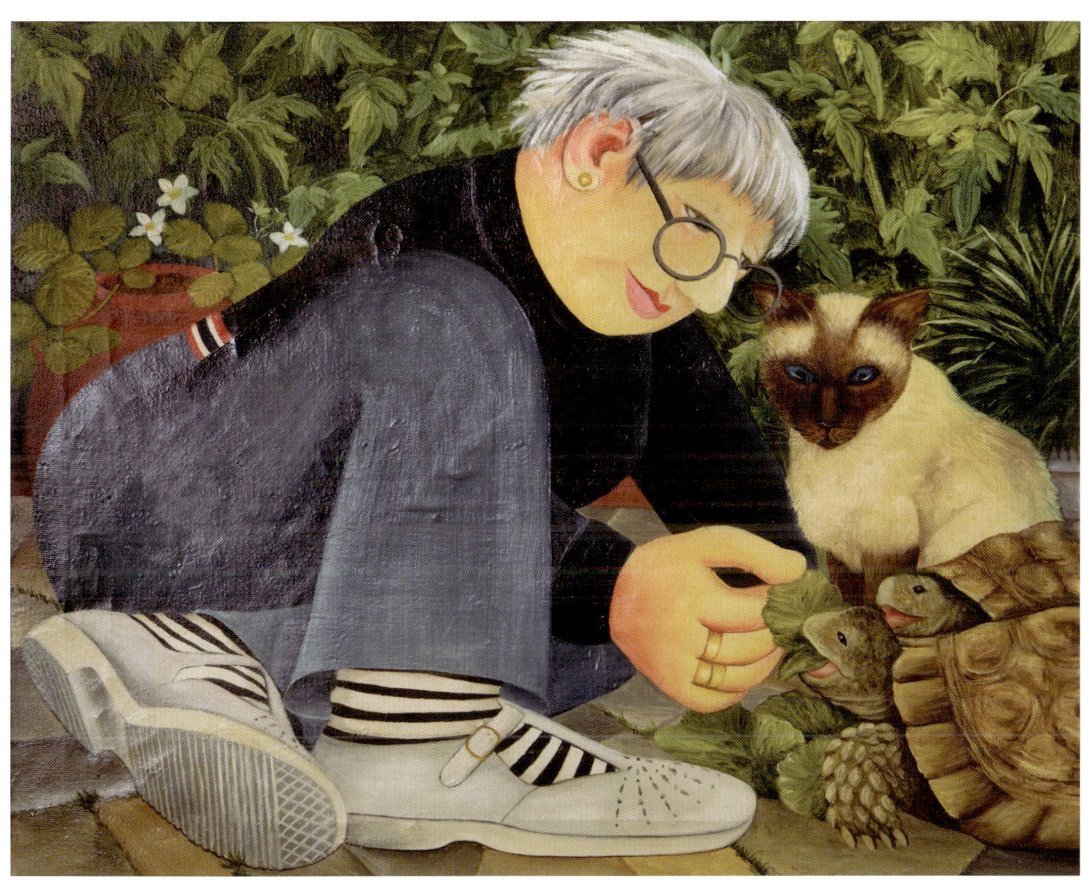

Feeding the Tortoises
circa 1974

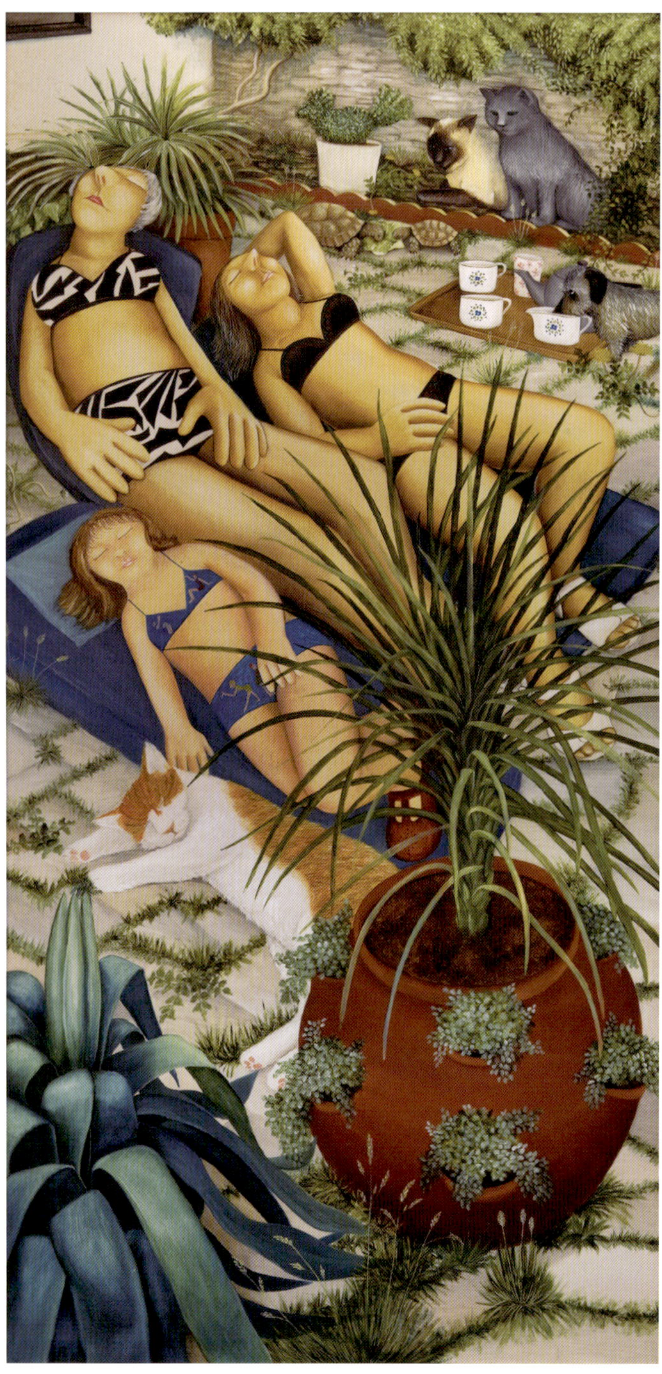

Sunbathing
circa 1974

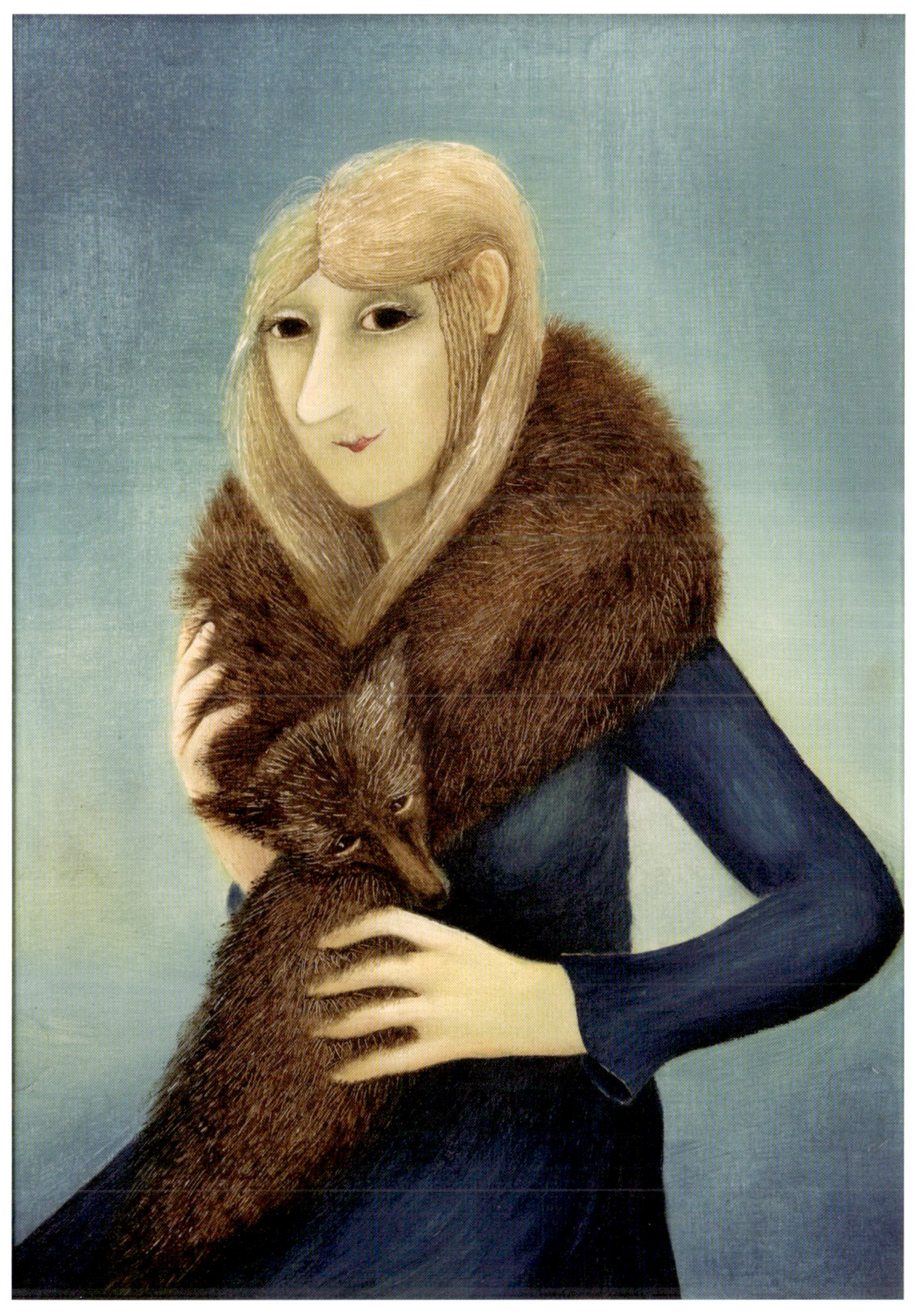

Teresa in a Fox Fur
circa 1974

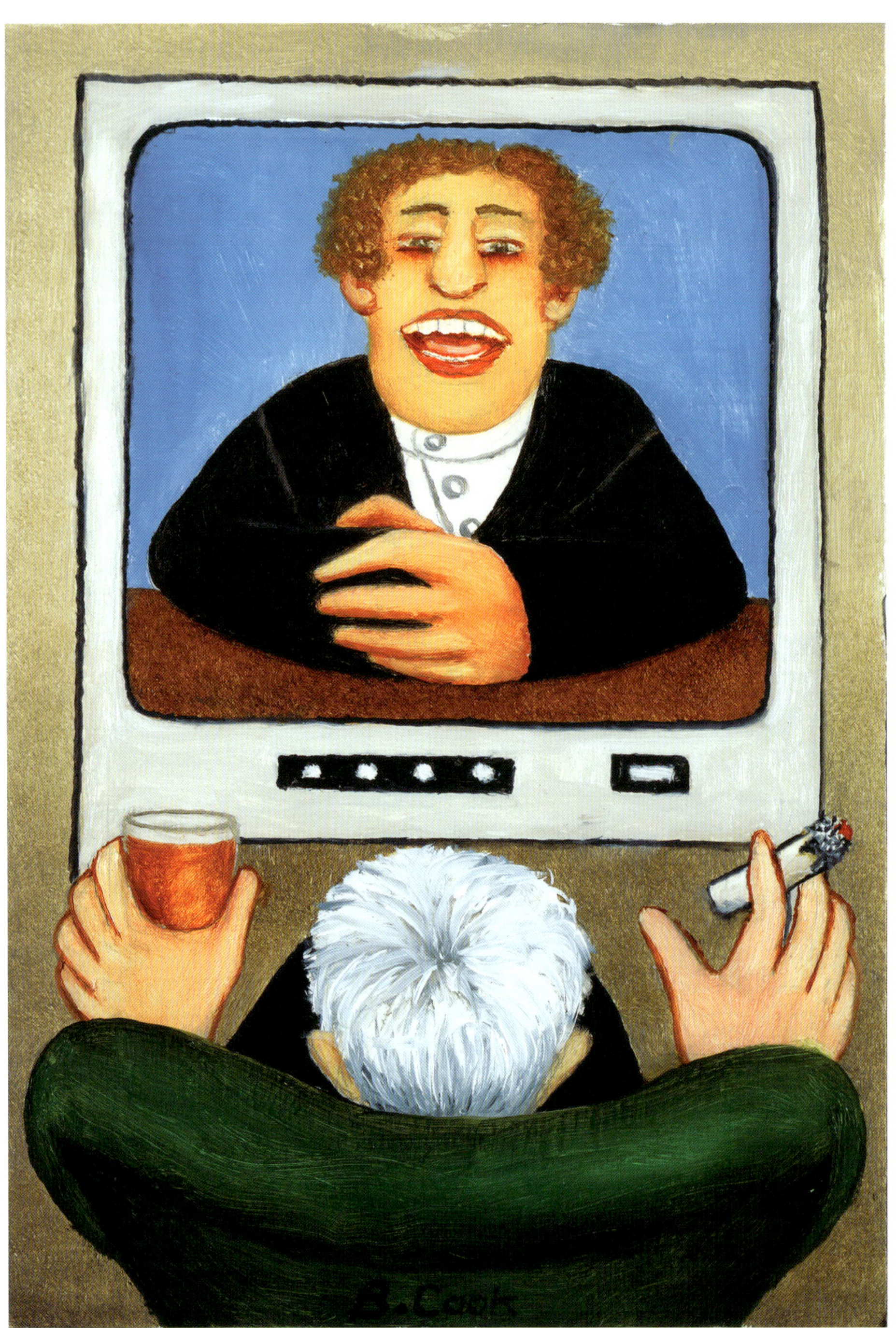

Talking about Art
2006

Heightened Reality

Edward Lucie-Smith

When Beryl Cook died, she was the subject of a large number of obituaries. Some of them were predictably condescending, which I suspect she would not have minded a bit. The really telling thing, however, is what has happened since then on the Web. If you go to the site maintained by *The Times*, still regarded as the British paper of record, and look for the paper's Obituary Archive, you will find a section within it devoted to 'Artistic Genius'. The subtitle is 'Artists and makers who changed the way we see'. And what is the illustration that the site's designers have chosen to head this section? A self portrait by Beryl Cook.

Further down the computer screen are Robert Rauschenberg, Jörg Immendorf, Sol Lewitt, Bernard Meadows, Patrick Caulfield, Eduardo Paolozzi, Agnes Martin, Allan Kaprow, Nam June Paik, but Beryl lords it triumphantly over them all. Without, I think, actually meaning to tell us this, *The Times*, in its Internet incarnation, has made a valid point. Beryl was one of the most completely recognizable artists of her epoch – at any rate here in Britain.

I can vouch for this from personal experience. Like many art critics, I have a motley collection of paintings, drawings and photographs hanging on the walls of my flat. Many of my visitors are not denizens of the art world. Newcomers drift through my rooms. "I like this," they say. "Who did it?" Or "I couldn't live with that." Beryl's work elicits only one comment: "Oh, you've got a Beryl Cook."

One asks oneself how this has come about? There are several answers, more complex than they seem at first. The first is that Beryl's work presents people with scenes and incidents they think they know. Nevertheless, it is a heightened reality. The everyday world acquires hallucinatory quality. It is more itself in Beryl's paintings than it would be if we observed the people and incidents these portray with our own eyes. Part of Beryl's appeal, of course, is her irrepressible sense of humour, but there is also a feeling that the images are a quite serious commentary on the way people choose to live their lives. Like many artists, Beryl loved things that were on the margins of society, not quite integrated into the general mass.

A number of celebrated artists have possessed this quality. Beryl is often compared to the designer of seaside postcards, Donald McGill, and she certainly admired his work. Yet there are other comparisons to be made – to Stanley Spencer, for instance, whose work she also liked, and whose sense of pictorial design is in some respects comparable to hers. Other names can be cited as well. It is not ridiculous to compare her to the Colombian artist, Fernando Botero, not only because they both like painting rotund figures, but also because of their taste for raucous, sleazy, low-life jollity. I am thinking, here, of the series of paintings of brothels that Botero made in the 1970s, which are arguably his best works. Other names suggest themselves – sometimes simply for subject matter, Toulouse-Lautrec, for example, and aspects of Goya. Sometimes for subject matter and style linked together. It is not absurd, I think, to compare some of Beryl's compositions to the drawings of Thomas Rowlandson, among them his 'Exhibition Stare Case' with its mass of tumbling figures. Beryl's humour, like Rowlandson's, is politically incorrect. One reason perhaps, why so many of the pundits of our time can't stand her.

The success of Beryl's paintings is based on two things – a keen sense of observation and a highly refined feeling for pictorial design, surprising in an untrained artist. Concerning Beryl the observer I can offer personal testimony. On one occasion we were in a pub garden somewhere in north Devon. One of those places where they turn the kiddies out to play while the adults get on with a bit of serious drinking inside. Almost the only other inhabitants of this space were two very rumbustious children and a woman who might perhaps have been their grandmother. She looked a bit like the actress Hermione Gingold – high piled dyed-blond hair, long pendulous nose, caked white make-up, a slash of purple lipstick. When your eye strayed downwards you saw black patent leather shoes with rather sinister straps, and, as a final touch, a gold ankle chain. My uncharitable guess was that she must be the retired madam of a brothel, or, failing that, the proprietress of a very louche B & B.

Beryl, I could sense, was immediately fascinated. It was rather like seeing a good hunting dog pointing at a bird. Rather naughtily I said, "That's going to be a picture, isn't it?" The only response was a giggle. Sure enough, next time I visited, there was the painting, already complete.

The method Beryl used to create her pictures was personal to herself. She did not draw, in the sense that drawing is usually understood. Indeed, she drew much less than Francis Bacon, who claimed, it now seems untruthfully, that he never did so. She was rather secretive about how the paintings were actually made, but as far as I could make out she started by making a few very tentative pencil lines. These did not delineate figures, even in very simplified form, but established basic shapes and rhythms. If you look carefully at her paintings, what makes them work is the way the forms push and jostle – against each other, and also against the edges of the picture. Her most successful compositions have great kinetic energy. Beryl used to claim that she made her figures rotund so as not to have to fill in the background. In fact their rotundity is a source of pictorial energy. Botero uses the same device in his paintings.

Beryl, like her admired Stanley Spencer, was not interested in paint as a substance. Her paintings have no visible marks of the brush. First Rembrandt and Hals, then the masters of modern abstraction, have taught us to admire the manipulation of paint as a quality in itself. Yet the majority of the artists who go to make up the western tradition are not like this. Among the non-painterly painters are the Limbourg brothers, who created the greatest of all late medieval manuscripts, the *Très Riches Heures* (1412-1416), and Pieter Bruegel the Elder. I name these in particular because some of their subject-matter is quite close to Beryl's preferred themes – Bruegel in particular, with paintings like 'The Peasant Dance' (1568).

The thing that has imprinted these artists on the memory of our culture is the fact that they offer images of human lives that are being fully lived. One can say the same thing about a number of the paintings made by Beryl Cook.

Edward Lucie-Smith is internationally known as an art critic, historian, photographer and poet.

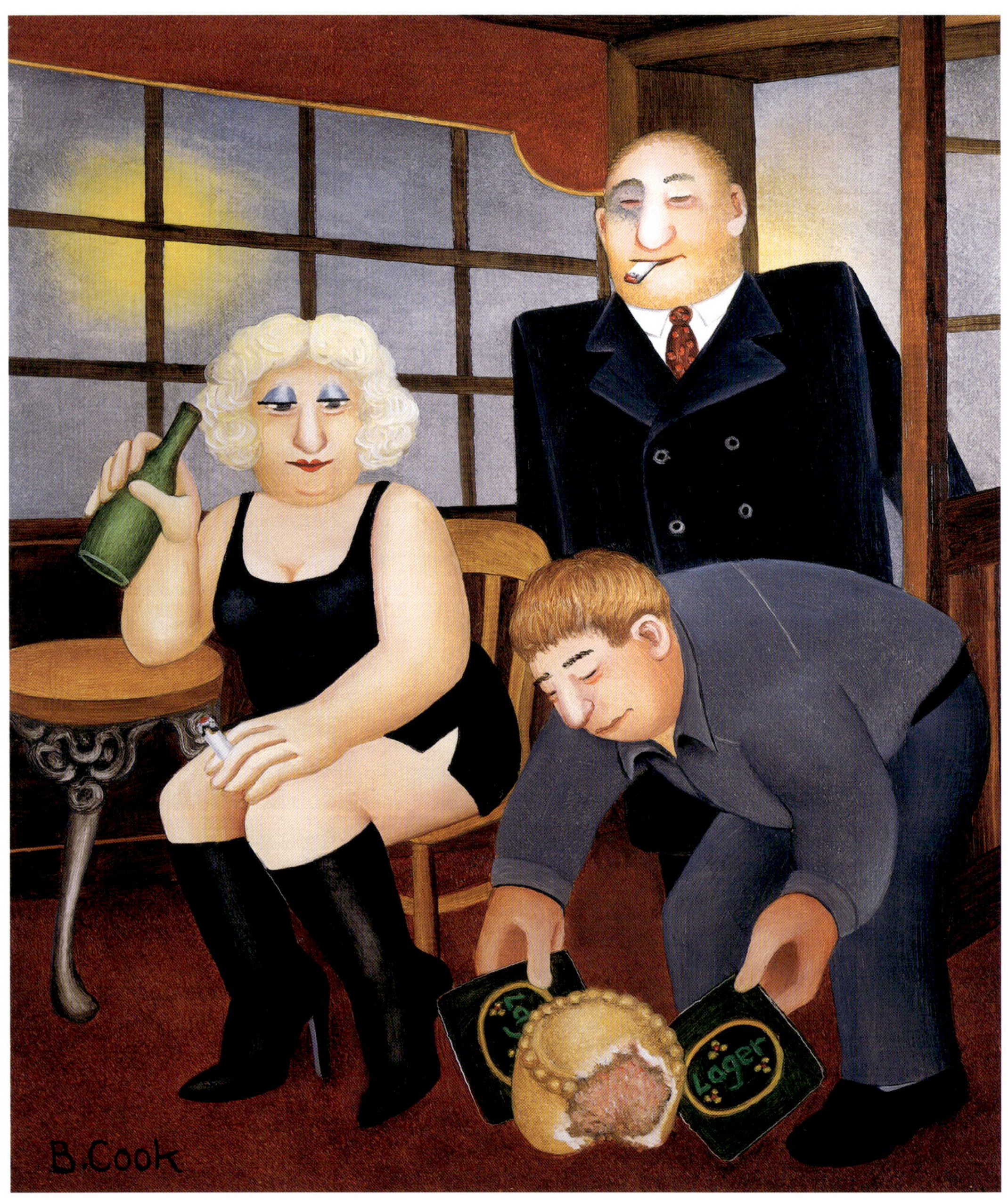

Interior with a Pork Pie
2000

Unruly Pleasures: Beryl Cook's popular appeal

Bernadette Casey

There is no doubt that Beryl Cook has, over a number of years, become a much loved figure within British popular culture. Her pictures have gained huge recognition and admiration from a public that extends well beyond the UK .[1] Whilst the paintings have sold well as originals, they have gained even more enormous success in their mass-reproduced, popular forms: greetings cards, prints, posters, calendars, illustrated books and so on. It is Cook's significance within popular culture, as well as the popular response to her work that will be the main focus of this essay. I intend to explore some inter-connecting themes, using concepts from cultural theory to open up debate about a range of ways in which we may experience Cook's work. Space is limited so I am going to concentrate on a small number of areas of discussion around the social context of Cook's work and on her representations of the body, particularly the female body. In doing so, I will utilize the concept of the 'carnivalesque'. In focusing on these areas, I will also include commentary on the divisions, actual and perceived, between Cook's critics and her admirers by examining directly some of the responses to her work.

In approaching Cook's work in this way, I want to challenge the often explicitly made assertion that Cook's art is at best a bit of fun and at worst worthless, and I want to contest the view, more implicitly held, that her fans are philistines or dopes. If we consider the work in its cultural and social context and if we think about the ways in which the work communicates, it is possible to regard

---

1 Postings on 'The Times Online' website in response to Cook's obituary in *The Times* included contributions from fans in Australia, the USA, Germany, Spain and Hungary, as well as from many parts of the UK. One Russian woman, posting from the USA, referred to her getting to know Cook's work via "a greetings card that somebody sneaked to Russia in the late 80s".

Beryl Cook's work and its reception as more complex and more significant than her critics allow.

On Beryl Cook's death in May 2008, many fans from all over the world contributed online responses to media obituaries. The fans' responses were united in their fondness and sorrow, but a number of them also made overt reference to their perception that Cook had been undervalued and sidelined by the art establishment. For instance:

> "I think all Beryl Cook's paintings are great…long may they live on! A truly English artist and shame she didn't get more recognition. Who cares – most people you speak to like her work so that's all that counts!! Good for you Beryl!" (Ian, Cologne)
>
> "I am absolutely devastated at this great loss to British culture. Yes I say culture, even if certain art galleries and critics looked down on her art" (Diane)
>
> "What a sad loss, my late wife and I both loved Beryl Cook's paintings... the Art Establishment could not recognize genius if it was the size of a London bus and ran over them" (Dennis)
>
> "She should have painted a picture of a big fat lady sticking two fingers up at the art world. A wonderful painter and cartoonist. RIP" (Grizelda)[2]

Given the strength of feeling expressed here, I feel it is important to consider the way in which Beryl Cook's work has been regarded in the art world. I do not intend to represent the division between 'fans' and 'the art world' as a monolithic entity or something unchanging and set in stone. Both of these labels would benefit from some interrogation: 'Beryl Cook fans' are not a unified or coherent group, even less so 'the art world', consisting as it does of many different and often conflicting interests. So I acknowledge that these terms can only be used as shorthand. I acknowledge too, the due attention that needs to be given to those individuals and organizations within the art

2 Quotes taken from the BBC Devon website, 'Have Your Say', downloaded 7 August 2008 and from 'The Times Online' in response to the obituary by Rachel Campbell-Johnston, chief Art Critic, also downloaded 7 August 2008.

world who spotted Cook's abilities and appeal many years ago. But even with these caveats, it is still easy to justify the claim that overall, Beryl Cook has not generally been highly regarded in art circles, despite her popularity with the general public.

To gain some insight here, it is worth noting that much of what has been written about Beryl Cook's work has focused on the question of whether or not she qualifies as an artist; in other words, whether her work is worthy to be called 'art'. It could be argued that this is an impossible question to resolve: it could also be noted that art critics may be at the point of re-evaluating her work, particularly since her death, but this is somewhat speculative. My point is that we need to shift the parameters of debate, to approach the subject of Cook's work from a different perspective than that of aesthetic evaluation in order to engage in another, potentially rich arena. However, Cook is ultimately judged in terms of her artistic abilities, it is undisputed that she has enjoyed commercial success. Indeed, it is arguably at least in part because of this success and her fan base that Beryl Cook's work has been largely dismissed and marginalized within the art world.

Cook's work takes the form of paintings, and the medium is of some significance, since painting is traditionally associated with 'high art'. All art, it may be argued, uses language, in this case visual language, to express, explain, describe and evaluate. But Cook was not tutored in the formal language of painting and in this sense, may be said to have used a kind of visual slang. Not only this, but she is known to have begun her painting using a children's set of paints and to have frequently painted on any surface that happened to be around, including old wardrobe doors, off-cuts and toilet seats. And she was modest and self deprecating. Hardly the classical route – no wonder substantial elements of the art world have been keen to dismiss her.

So, we need to re-think all this: what is it that makes her so popular, outside art circles? What are the dimensions of her appeal? Conventional accounts are generally simplistic and often disparaging, explaining her popularity away by a lowest common denominator factor. They more than hint that people who like Beryl Cook's work are an inferior breed and know nothing about art. Apart from Brian Sewell's accusation that the work is no more than a "very successful formula which fools are prepared to buy",[3] others have joined in a similar, familiar refrain. For instance, Adrian Searle in *The Guardian* wrote of Cook's exhibition at the Baltic in 2007:

> "…her art depresses me…the best that can be said is that Cook celebrates ordinariness…she makes art for people who don't much like art, which is fine…Say no to Cook and you are an illiberal, snobbish bore, with no sense of fun. After all, everyone likes a bit of rubbishy art now and again." [4]

More kindly and sympathetic, but engaging in a similar discourse, is this passage from the obituary by Veronica Horwell in May 2008, where she describes how the artist would go shopping in Plymouth then come home to paint:

> "...to record the great times she had witnessed. This involved two weeks of drawing and painting on marine three-ply board, two foot by three, starting at the top and rushing forward to 'the whopping great figure in the foreground'. After the first two days, she said, there always came the realization that the work would be a dud. But she finished it anyway."[5]

Each of these to varying degrees, emphasize Cook's (lack of) skill as judged by artistic measures and two of them make negative assumptions about the judgmental capabilities of her fans. Both Cook and her admirers are seen as somehow 'lacking'...

Cook's paintings are visual artifacts, or texts, but they work both as an embodiment and an interpretation of lived culture. The meaning of texts is never fixed, but is formed through interaction with a viewer, reader or audience. However, there may be dominant understandings at play and these particular texts, though apparently innocent and transparent (often described as 'humorous', 'cheeky' and 'saucy'), mask a complexity about the world and

---

3 Cited in Veronica Horwell's obituary, *The Guardian*, 28 May 2008.

4 Adrian Searle, *The Guardian*, July 24 2007.

5 Horwell, V, 28 May 2008, as above.

roles and relationships within it. They are very much open to a range of 'ways of seeing' and understanding, but establishing a range of possible meanings can involve a process of struggle, or contestation. In the case of Cook's work, the 'contest' – between fans and critics – is, as we have seen, sometimes quite explicit.

I would like to link this with a discussion about social context and specifically to say something about the significance of this context in Beryl Cook's work. The city and people of Plymouth feature strongly in many of her paintings. Although Cook began painting before moving to the city, it was in Plymouth that she was 'discovered' and where she first exhibited and received some encouragement and acclaim. Importantly, the pictures from her time in Plymouth are the ones that are most familiar, and which made her famous: people who have never visited Plymouth are nevertheless *au fait* with The Dolphin pub, Union St. and the Barbican. The pictures therefore set a particular tone, not only for her work but for the popular recognition Cook received. Plymouth is a working (class) city and remains so despite some recent demographic and economic changes. It is now becoming a little more diverse, though it is still ethnically and culturally narrow for an urban area of its size. It appears also to have resisted attempts to make it more gentrified and middle class, even though there have been, and continue to be, many ambitious educational, commercial and civic projects designed to upgrade it. Plymouth still feels geographically peripheral despite improving communications and it can seem a long way from where the action is. Certainly, in terms of art, the 'scene' remains predominantly elsewhere – in London, in certain parts of Cornwall and Devon, but not really in Plymouth. That's not to say there are no artists here; simply that they are to some extent shaped and maybe disadvantaged by cultural geography.

However, all this is key to Plymouth's and Beryl Cook's appeal. What could be described as a 'lack' in Plymouth's cultural scene (and as suggested above, in Cook and her fans) can be turned on its head – Plymouth's very grittiness, its dockyard-and-seaside-ness, its slightly down-at-heel post-war appearance, its reputation for toughness, are exactly those things that are positively valued in Beryl Cook's pictures. For many Plymothians and, we have to assume, for Cook herself, the appeal of Plymouth is in its less conventionally respectable or certainly less up-market face. This appeal begins with Plymouth but does not end there. Beryl Cook's depictions of the city and its people are popular, way beyond the locality, and her later work shows scenes from further afield – though usually these are places that would allow her to observe and capture similar elements.

It is not enough to simply state that Cook paints people having fun, as has so often been the basic comment, but that she paints particular kinds of people having particular kinds of fun. What kinds of people? Well an initial look shows us that they are almost always people who need to work for a living. I am hesitant to use the term 'working class' here because in twenty first century Britain this is too crude and narrow a descriptor, but equally the term 'popular class(es)', often used in cultural theory, is too broad and does not quite capture Cook's world. Whilst we do occasionally see what might be described as genteel, refined people in her pictures, they are rare. More often her subjects are women and men who dress up and go out but only after a hard day's (or night's) work. They are shop assistants and office workers, bouncers and sailors, prostitutes, pub workers, housewives and retirees. They walk on the Hoe, go to Woolworth's for sweets, drink outside pubs on a sunny day and inside pubs any night of the week. They get into taxis, dance, go to the cinema, play bingo and stride out loudly on hen nights. Sometimes their pursuits verge on the lewd, but just as often they are 'respectable' activities like walking the dog, gardening or trying on shoes. They are just as likely to be middle-aged or older as young, and probably stout rather than slim – and they don't care. It is their world, and they are cheerfully proud of it.

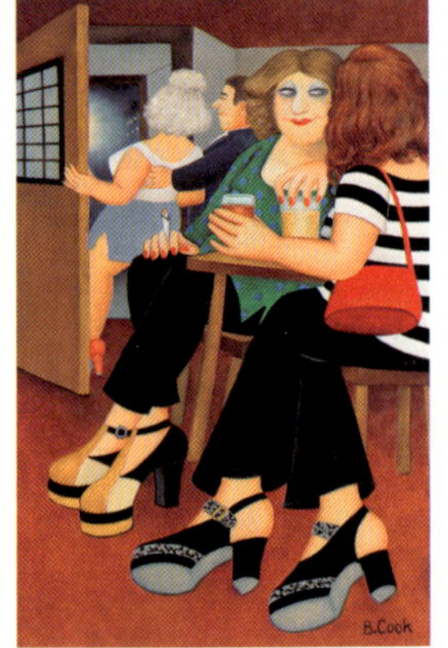

Fig. 11 Beryl Cook
Big Shoes
Oil on panel
Private collection

It would be unwise to attribute to Beryl Cook any rebellious, let alone politically radical, intention, but her pictures nevertheless show us, and speak for, groups within society that may be in the majority but are not culturally dominant. They do not hold the lion's share of power, wealth or what the French social theorist, Pierre Bourdieu called 'cultural capital'.[6] Their social context is circumscribed by economic and cultural status but they are not defined by it. Bourdieu described how notions of 'taste' are intrinsically linked to cultural capital, in other words how those with the greatest cultural capital are able to define what is 'good' and 'bad' taste and try to impose their (dominant) values

6 Bourdieu, P. *Distinction: A Social Critique of the Judgement of Taste*. London: Routledge and Kegan Paul, 1984 (originally published in 1979)

onto the taste preferences of others. The habitual aspects of everyday life – or 'habitus' in Bourdieu's terminology - 'place' us in a hierarchy defined by the cultural framework and used by the powerful to define themselves as different from, and better than, the powerless. (Drinking champagne at Ascot is one thing, whilst drinking cider in the underpass is quite another). Yet Cook's characters, far from passively accepting this set of symbolic values, are actively engaged in carving out their own lives, creating positive meanings, asserting their own tastes. One of the most iconic Cook images, 'Sabotage', sums up this attitude. The picture shows three women bowlers, one of whom is poking her finger up another one's bottom as she bends towards her ball to take her turn. The woman doing the 'goosing' looks straight out at the observer with a knowing and somewhat defiant look on her face. Of course it is 'playful' and includes an element of fantasy, but this picture, like many more from Cook's body of work, is firmly based in a specific kind of reality and comes from a recognizable habitus. It is not 'good taste', but it holds great appeal for those who can relate to its insolence and insubordination. A similar interpretation can be made of any number of Cook's pictures, such as 'The Lockyer Tavern', 'My Fur Coat' or 'Girls in a Taxi'. It cannot be a coincidence either that Cook's pictorial world is also her own world, viewed from the inside, not condescendingly from the outside. She pays tribute to older, ordinary, not particularly beautiful women (and men) just by making them visible in a way that is fond and not mocking.

This is a useful jumping-off point for thinking about Cook's representations of the body, especially the female body, which has been so central a part of Cook's work and the responses to it. One of the most recognisable elements within Cook's paintings, arguably her 'trademark', remains her 'fat ladies'. But I would argue that the size, shape and sometimes the age, of her female figures are key components in what I have already described as a cultural struggle for meaning. The predominant western cultural norm in terms of body size and shape is one that celebrates thinness and abhors fatness. Large people, and especially large women, are for the most part regarded as not only unattractive but also unhealthy. They are increasingly blamed for being too lazy to slim down and for putting a strain on the nation's public health resources. This attitude, prevalent in popular texts of all kinds and within medical and political discourse, is of course historically and socially relative, but it has escalated in contemporary western societies into a moral panic wherein obesity has become the new 'folk devil'. Obese people are now regarded as transgressive and 'out of control'. Beryl Cook had an obvious eye for humans with a good deal of flesh; although she is often quoted as explaining her large figures in terms of filling up the space so as not to have to paint backgrounds, she is also on record as stating a preference for 'large'. So there is a tension between Cook's popularity and the widespread cultural value placed on slimness. Why do fans love Cook's large figures, when so little value is placed on them in 'real life'?

To try to answer this, I would like to explore connections between Cook's body shapes and the appeal of carnival and the carnivalesque, by referring to the writings of Mikhail Bakhtin, the Russian writer of the 1920s and 1930s.[7] Although this seems a huge leap to make in order to throw some light on Beryl Cook's paintings, Bakhtin's ideas about the significance of the body in carnival can in fact be helpful here. For Bakhtin, elements of pre-industrial carnival are still in evidence in the modern world. Carnival was and is a ritual whereby all acceptable norms and boundaries of behaviour are given a temporary holiday. Carnival is not only a celebration of pleasure, it is transgressive in disregarding normal constraints ('the world turned upside-down'). Very significantly, the pleasures of carnival are overwhelmingly corporeal. They are physical rather than spiritual, exaggerated and vulgar rather than refined. The physicality of carnival is concentrated on what he calls 'grotesque realism' – figures with huge breasts, stomachs and buttocks, often still seen in carnival parades – and it is an opportunity to ritually celebrate bodily indulgence. If we think about contemporary carnivals such as (Gay) Pride events all over the world, Mardi Gras in New Orleans or the Notting Hill Carnival in the UK, they are opportunities for excess in all its cultural (and very clearly, physical) forms, including music, dance, drinking and sexual display, often through revealing and outrageous costumes, and cross dressing. Some of these events emerge too from an assertion of the right to be seen and heard by minority groups of one kind or another. Policing is always more than evident at carnival, because in an atmosphere of assertion and excess, the potential for 'breaking loose' is palpable. However, the most crucial element of carnival is that it is temporary. License is granted but only for a defined period.

---

7 Bakhtin, M. *Rabelais and His World*, Bloomington, IN: Indiana University Press, 1984 (originally published in English, 1968).

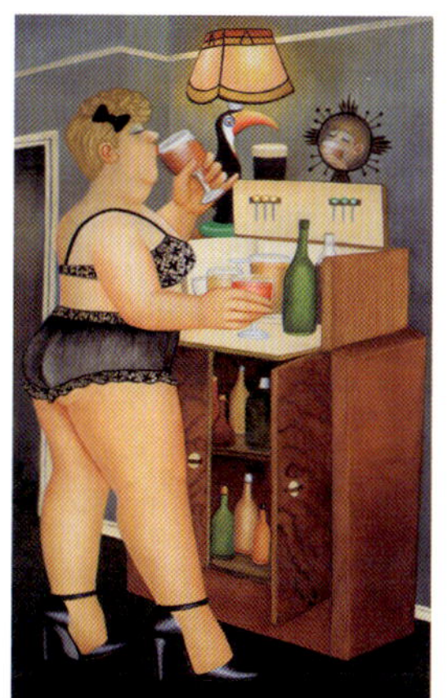

Fig. 12 Beryl Cook
Drinkies
Oil on panel
Private collection

Many of Beryl Cook's figures, and her women most especially, look like they are permanently in carnival mode. The large, rounded figures, shown off by tight, short clothing ('Lady of Marseilles', 'Girls in a Taxi', 'Satin Dresses') or emphasized by the angle from which they are depicted ('Staircase', 'Bus Stop'), embody a spirit of defiance and excess. The adage 'you can never be too rich or too thin' is not so much meaningless in Cook's pictures as irrelevant, both in the world of the characters and in the world inhabited by many of Cook's fans. So the appeal of Cook's rounded figures may be at least partially explained as a kind of symbolic, imaginary resolution of tensions between the everyday, rule-bound world (where we strive to be healthier and thinner and we get on with our jobs) and an unobtainable, yet recognisable 'carnival' world, where we can celebrate the imperfections that make us human, within a free and easy atmosphere. Most of us may not ever play strip poker or dress in drag but with Cook's pictures, we can visualise a situation where we might! In 'Birthday Surprises', a picture commissioned by British Rail, Cook depicted a typically rotund, older female figure, dressed in a scanty two-piece and high heels (described by Cook herself as "suitable gear for the fun-loving older woman") emerging from a cake clutching a senior citizen rail card[8]. For me, this image epitomizes the sense of symbolic inversion that runs through Cook's work in that it combines a cheerful acceptance of getting older with an element of unruly behaviour.

Interestingly, Beryl Cook painted a picture based on the Plymouth Carnival (or Lord Mayor's procession, as it is now more respectably called). In her 1991 book, *Bouncers*, Cook describes how she came to paint the picture 'Carnival in Plymouth'. The picture features a woman in a bright costume, lounging on the bonnet of a moving police car. Cook relates how a police officer told her about offering a worn-out carnival performer a lift, whereupon she promptly laid herself out on the bonnet. Whether or not Cook had ever heard of Bakhtin, she was certainly tuned in to his ideas, showing us here in her characteristically humorous fashion, the carnival spirit of license and its relationship with law and order.

It seems then that through her paintings Cook communicates a recognition of the minutiae of everyday life, whilst also suggesting underlying, perhaps unspoken, desires and fantasies. This seems to be a rare talent, based on acute

8 'Birthday Surprises' and Cook's commentary on it is to be found in her book *Bouncers*, London: Victor Gollancz, 1991.

social sensitivity and observation. Although the paintings are not 'realistic' in style, they nevertheless, in their subject matter, settings and characters, offer a fidelity to reality that is a large part of their appeal. In walking through Plymouth city centre, as I frequently do, I am often moved to think that Beryl Cook's figures are really not an exaggeration at all – they are all there in plain view. So it is perhaps fitting to conclude by giving the last word to Cook's fans.

> "Anyone who loves Beryl's work should visit Plymouth. I don't think there is anywhere quite like it and she's captured its essence perfectly. Women of a certain age are much loved and a highly visible presence on the streets here." (DM)
>
> "The real joy of life observed and preserved." (Jim)[9]

Bernadette Casey writes on media and popular culture. She is Dean of Culture, Communication and Society, University College Plymouth St Mark & St John.

9 'The Times Online' and BBC Devon websites, as above.

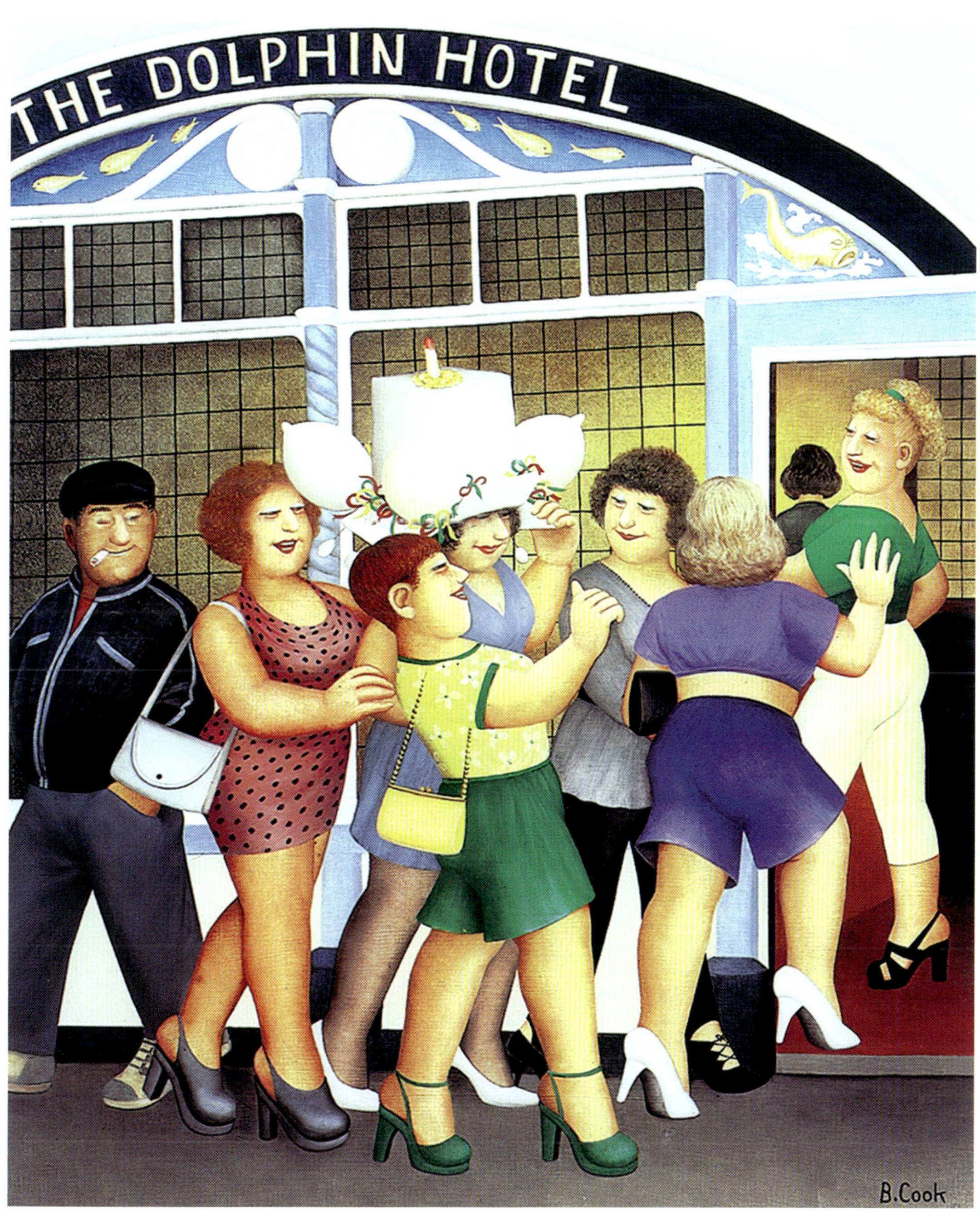

Hen Party 1
1995

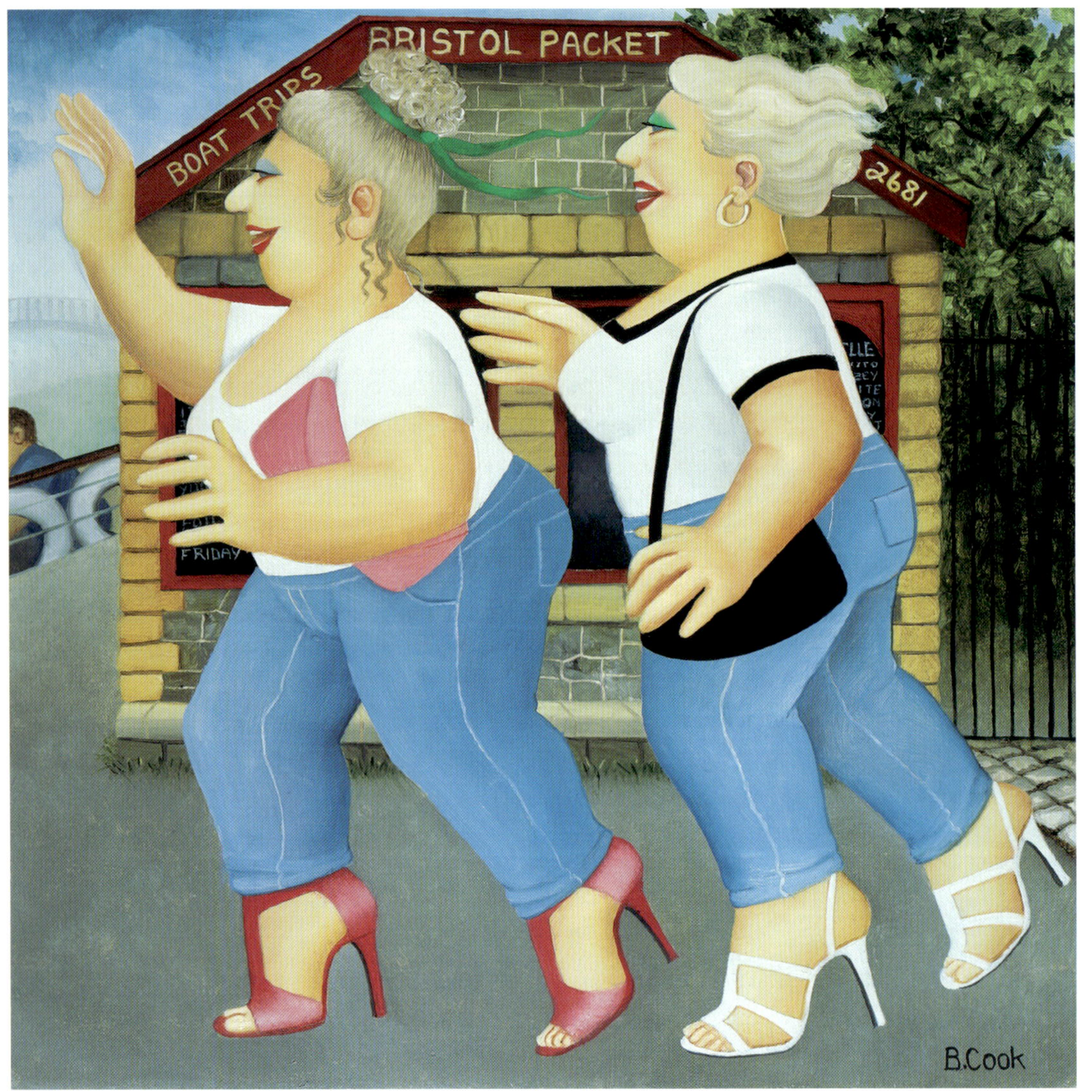

Ahoy There!
2003

LIFE WITH LAUGHTER

Babs Horton

I first found a Beryl Cook card in a shop in Plymouth many years ago. I stared down at it in fascination, laughed out loud and bought it for my sister's birthday because I knew instinctively that as an artist she would appreciate Beryl's work. My sister was duly delighted, Beryl Cook became a firm family favourite and we rejoiced in her success and growing fame. The card that gave me such delight was called 'Sabotage'. Bowls had always seemed so staid and boring to me up until that point. 'Sabotage' was a picture of three ladies on a bowling green, one lady poking her opponent unceremoniously up the behind in an attempt to put her off her stroke. I have often tried to put my own finger on exactly what it is about Beryl Cook's work that has enthralled me for so many years. I think it is because she was able to infuse an absolute joy and vitality into all her colourful work. She captured wickedness, mischief, the *joie de vivre* that was all around her in the pubs, clubs, cafés and open spaces of Plymouth. Beryl was a keen observer of life, had a sharp eye for detail and knew how to prick pomposity with her paintbrush and give us all a good time. Beryl effortlessly exaggerated her characters and captured so many lovely moments for all of us to share.

If I stare for a long time at her pictures I can conjure up conversations between her characters, can hear the sound of their high heels clattering as they teeter across the damp cobbles of the Barbican, the tinkling of glasses in The Dolphin and the raucous unbridled laughter on the night air. I can smell the beer, the hairspray and the perfume, the sweat and the mingling of cigarette smoke. Beryl Cook was a wonderful, eccentric individual, a talented artist who saw the world with a wry sense of humour and was able to translate her vision and communicate with the public. She took everyday scenes of Plymouth and its people, images which would otherwise be forgotten but which were and are familiar to all who frequent the Barbican and bars of Plymouth. The colour and fun of her work is attractive to the eye and uplifting to the spirits.

Her paintings are a celebration of the life lived by ordinary people. Her women are truly memorable. They are wonderful, glamorous, voluptuous and deliciously loud, no shrinking violets here. They are big busted, big bottomed, big hearted people in a big hearted city. Beryl's subjects were not the size zero type of woman that our society so admires these days; the stick thin celebrities who send out a warped message to young, impressionable girls everywhere. Not for Beryl the voluntarily starving, lettuce munching skeleton slumped over a skinny latte. Her women were big, buxom girls who didn't need makeover programmes, such as the current British television series with Trinny and Susannah, to stuff them into magic knickers or instil them with confidence and the approval to go out and have fun. These were bold and unbowed girls, bursting with curiosity and energy. The very sight of the dimpled thighs and heaving bosoms would be enough to give the British TV presenter and author Gillian McKeith[1] and Health Ministers heart palpitations and make health freaks choke on their sushi. These were girls brimming with life, girls up for fun on their own terms, knowing that life is short but that the night is young. For me Beryl's energy and sense of humour are an antidote to the succession of governments who have told us what to do, what to eat, to read, what to feed our children, steadily diluting our lives, our art and our culture.

There continues to be much snobbery about literature and art. I recently heard someone urging their son to fill his bookshelves with 'good' literature even if he didn't read it, in order to impress his visitors. How sad is that?

One thing I loved about Beryl Cook was that she came to the world of art quite late in life. Middle age can be a time when many women feel that they are becoming anonymous, burned out and invisible. A time when they might as well give up and concentrate on the joys awaiting them, the exciting day when you fit snugly into your first pair of incontinence pants, take a ride serenely up and down on a Stannah stair lift in search of your spectacles. A few weeks ago a man said to me that sadly writing groups were full of middle-aged women – as if it were a crime for them to search out new activities and explore their creativity. However much we women have to care and nurture, most of us can't say that washing other people's underwear and cleaning the skirting boards is exactly uplifting and creative.

---

1 Gillian McKeith, *You Are What You Eat*. London: Michael Joseph Ltd, 2004.

How energetically Beryl ran with her newly discovered talent and grasped at life. How she rejoiced in finding and exploring her talents and in doing so brought joy to thousands. When other women were giving up she carved for herself a new career and a place in the hearts and minds of so many. Indeed, Beryl was a beacon of inspiration to women of a certain age everywhere. Certainly she gave me new hope when I began writing. Her story of success inspired many to keep going against all the odds and discrimination. When I was published at 49 I danced and wobbled and celebrated vigorously, just as her lively women did.

Of course there are those in the art establishment who have very set views on what kind of art is acceptable for public consumption. The role of these gatekeepers is performed with diligence and determination whenever any artist steps out of the accepted mould. Seemingly a painting must be complex, capable of being discussed in the minutest detail. It must be analysed to ascertain the artist's aim, the hidden meanings, etc. A painting must not be common unless it's 'an unmade bed' or 'a tin of tomato soup'. The guardians of the artistic taste of this country are guilty of admiring and applauding the court photographer, Vermeer, and the bad boys, Damien Hurst, Tracey Emin, *et al.* Whilst I believe all these artists hold a well deserved place in the public domain, I am saddened that such a vibrant talent as Beryl Cook could be ignored for so long. Many of the great and the good tell us that Beryl's work is not good art; in fact one poor fellow was made to feel 'queasy' by her work. Are these folk not implying that if we like her work we are under educated and not capable of knowing the difference between great art and poor art.Their disdain is palpable; many of them sound so horrified and would most likely don latex gloves in case they had to make contact with the working classes. I, one of the great unwashed, applaud Beryl wholeheartedly. They can keep their snobbery, their disdain and high mindedness. They may choose not to hang her work in the Tate but her fans will continue to view her work and travel miles to do so.

Over the years I have appreciated many different works of art in galleries around the world. I've appreciated them for a variety of reasons – skill, content, feeling, novelty – the list is endless, but I have enjoyed only a few. The wonderful 'talking' statues of Juan Munoz, the revolving humming proboscis in the Pompidou Centre, shamefully I forget the artist's name now. Always my favourite, Toulouse Lautrec had so much in common with Beryl Cook, they both took the everyday activities of their contemporaries and translated them to canvas, driftwood and paper in all the vibrant colour and humour of the time. In both artists' work it is possible to hear the noise and colour of the Moulin Rouge and the Barbican in all their festive glory.

Beryl Cook was an extraordinary woman, a woman brimming with humanity. She was skilled and talented and able to see the comic side of life in most things and her interpretation of situations was unique. The general public recognised her genuine integrity and authenticity in all her work and she holds a place of affection in many people's hearts.

In my view, a Beryl Cook painting is a veritable feast for the eyes and a kickstart for the soul. One can revel in the glorious detail and individuality of her characters, the vibrant colours and the vim and verve of her execution, her lack of pretension and her humanity. She gives the viewer an abundance of delight and joy on all that life has to offer, whatever our size, whatever our peccadilloes.

If there is an afterlife, I imagine a rosy cheeked Beryl perched on a fluffy cloud skilfully depicting the chubby buttocks of an angel, the wry wink of a beefy St Peter.

> Wherever you are Beryl Cook have a drink on me.
> Life without you has much less laughter.
> I miss you.

Babs Horton, novelist, prize-winning writer, Royal Literary Fund Writing Fellow at the University of Plymouth and former teacher, lives and work in Plymouth. www.babshorton.co.uk

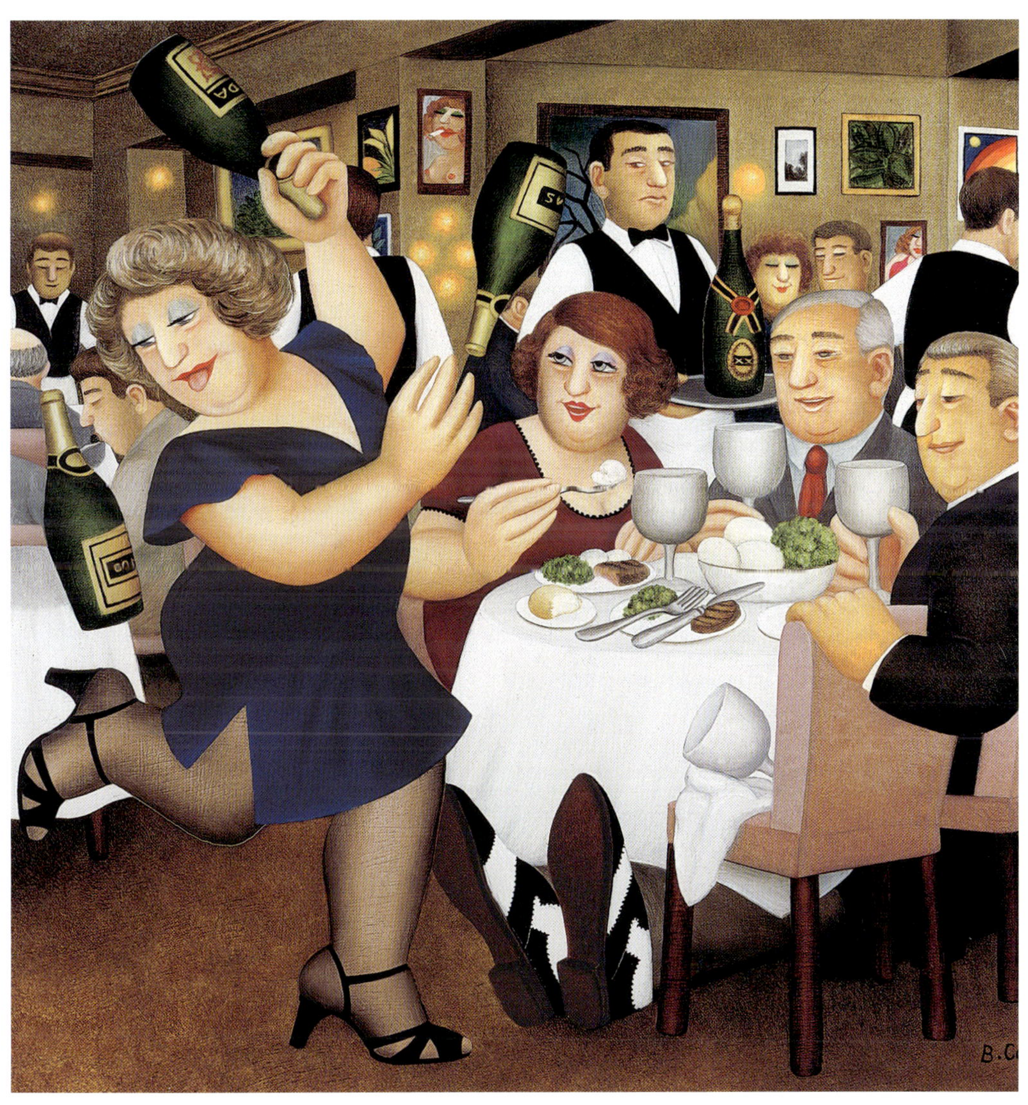

Dining Out
1994

PICTURE LIST

Acknowledgements

In working on this exhibition and book I wish to thank the Cook family who have been generously supportive of this project throughout. Significantly Beryl herself, before her sad death earlier this year, was very excited at the prospect of having a major exhibition in the city that inspired so much of her imagery.

Very many thanks are due to Jess Wilder, co-director of Portal Gallery, London, whose passionate support of Beryl's work for some 30 years has been pivotal to the sourcing and collation of the entire project. I must also thank all those who lent work for the exhibition and for inclusion in this publication, and, most particularly, the contributing writers who have examined and reassessed Beryl's unique contribution to British Art. Thanks are also extended to Frank Larkin from Gallery Five, Bristol, for his time and generosity in supplying many of the images for this book and to Norman Henry of Flanigan Graphics (New Jersey, USA). Norman is responsible for all of Beryl's silkscreen prints and who has helped promote her reputation internationally.

It is important to acknowledge the University of Plymouth for its ongoing commitment to the Arts, in particular Professor Mary Watkins, Deputy Vice-Chancellor, whose early support for the exhibition was critical. Within the Faculty of Arts I should like to acknowledge the contribution and support of Simon Ible (Director), Sarah Honywill and Katie Mitchell within the Peninsula Arts team, and Mike Endicott and Keith Spears within the Faculty's technical team. I would also like to thank Paul Honeywill, Managing Director, University of Plymouth Press, for his commitment to this publication.

Finally, I wish to acknowledge the expertise, knowledge and encouragement of Liz Wells who, in addition to chairing the Peninsula Arts Galleries Programming Advisory Group, has taken a special interest in this publication from the outset; her insight and advice have been invaluable and especially appreciated.

Sarah Chapman
Peninsula Arts Gallery
November, 2008.